CONTENTS

Introduction

Confronting Child Abuse is the twenty-second volume in the **Issues** series. The aim of this series is to offer up-to-date information about important issues in our world.

Confronting Child Abuse examines child abuse and paedophilia.

The information comes from a wide variety of sources and includes:
Government reports and statistics
Newspaper reports and features
Magazine articles and surveys
Literature from lobby groups
and charitable organisations.

It is hoped that, as you read about the many aspects of the issues explored in this book, you will critically evaluate the information presented. It is important that you decide whether you are being presented with facts or opinions. Does the writer give a biased or an unbiased report? If an opinion is being expressed, do you agree with the writer?

Confronting Child Abuse offers a useful starting-point for those who need convenient access to information about the many issues involved. However, it is only a starting-point. At the back of the book is a list of organisations which you may want to contact for further information.

*****

Confronting Child Abuse

ISSUES
(formerly Issues for the Nineties)

Volume 22

Editor

Craig Donnellan

Independence
Educational Publishers
Cambridge

First published by Independence
PO Box 295
Cambridge CB1 3XP
England

British Library Cataloguing in Publication Data
Confronting Child Abuse – (Issues Series)
I. Donnellan, Craig II. Series
362.7'6

ISBN 1 86168 178 X

Printed in Great Britain
The Burlington Press
Cambridge

Typeset by
Claire Boyd

Cover
The illustration on the front cover is by
Pumpkin House.

Child abuse

Information from CHILDREN 1st

What is child abuse?

There are four main types of abuse: *Physical Abuse* is where children are hurt or injured by parents or others. It includes hitting, kicking and beating. These can cause pain, cuts, bruising, broken bones and sometimes even death.

Emotional Abuse includes sarcasm, degrading punishment, threats and not giving love and attention. All of which can undermine a child or young person's confidence.

Neglect occurs when children's basic needs such as food, warmth and medical care are not met by their parents.

Sexual Abuse occurs when children are forced or persuaded into sexual acts or situations by others.

Is there more child abuse now?

Throughout history there has always been cruelty towards children. Many of the national children's organisations were founded at the end of the nineteenth century; RSSPCC, the NSPCC, Save the Children, Barnardo's. They were created to deal with the problems of child neglect, child destitution, children begging etc. What has happened in recent years is not necessarily that there is more abuse, but that we have become more aware of it.

It is often said that child abuse was 'rediscovered' in the late 1960s/early 1970s. In America in 1962, Henry Kempe, a paediatrician, described the 'battered baby syndrome'. Kempe suggested that baby battering existed on a much larger scale than had previously been recognised. As a result of his work, doctors became more skilled in recognising the physical signs of abuse.

In 1973 an inquiry was held into the death of Maria Colwell. Maria, aged 7, had been killed by her

stepfather after being returned home from care. The tragedy attracted much media attention and brought child abuse firmly to the attention of the public.

Who abuses children?

There is no typical child abuser. In most cases of child abuse, the child knows the abuser. It may be a member of the child's family or a friend of the family. It is less common for a stranger to abuse a child. Child abuse can happen in any kind of family. Research shows that:

- over 90% of child sexual abusers are men
- less than 25% of abused children are sexually abused by strangers.[1]

What are the effects of child abuse?

Child abuse can cause physical injury, but can also leave emotional scars. And children may have difficulties because of the abuse. Abuse can lead to low self-esteem; children often blame themselves for it. In later life adults abused as children may find it difficult to form relationships because they are unable to trust people. All forms of abuse have a damaging effect on children and young people.

How many children are abused?

In Scotland in the year ending March 1999, just over 7,300 children were referred to local authorities for child protection enquiries.

When an investigation is conducted and the child is thought to be at risk of abuse, they are put on the Child Protection Register. 2,361 children were on the Child Protection Register in Scotland at March 1999. The most common reason was for physical abuse or injury.

Official figures underestimate the number of children abused. For example, children abused may not come to the notice of social workers,

either because they have not told anyone about it, or no one has reported it. Official statistics could be said to represent the tip of the iceberg.

Physical Abuse – One estimate is that each year 150,000 children in the UK are harmed by severe physical assaults.[2] Physical abuse is often a result of excessive physical punishment by a parent.

Sexual Abuse – Figures for the number of children sexually abused also vary considerably. The National Commission into the Prevention of Child Abuse *estimated* that up to 100,000 children each year have a potentially harmful sexual experience.[3] But the actual extent is unknown.

Emotional Abuse and Neglect – Emotional abuse and neglect are sometimes harder to define than physical or sexual abuse. However, it is clear that emotional abuse and neglect are equally harmful. Often a child is the victim of multiple abuse, for example, if they are physically abused there is a high chance that they are also emotionally abused.

The Child Protection Register shows that more boys are victims of physical abuse and neglect while more girls are victims of sexual abuse.

What happens when a child tells someone they are being abused?

Anyone can contact the police or social work department if they think that a child is being abused. The social work department will always investigate an allegation of abuse. A case conference may be called.

A case conference is a meeting of all the different agencies who may be involved with the child and may therefore have relevant information. It can include the social worker for the child and family, doctors, teachers, health visitors, the police and nursery staff.

The case conference will consider all the circumstances and assess the risk to the child. The child may be placed on the Child Protection Register if there is risk of abuse.

In most cases, children can continue to live at home with their family. Only in the most extreme situations will it be necessary to go to

---

The facts

- At least one child dies every week following abuse and neglect.
- Around 36,000 children are on child protection registers.
- A Home Office study showed that 26% of all recorded rape victims were children.
- 350,000 to 400,000 children live in families which are 'consistently low in warmth and high in criticism'.
- 15% of 8-11-year-olds said that they would not talk to anyone if they had a problem.
- About one-third of girls and over one-fifth of boys (aged between 12 and 15) said they were afraid, at least sometimes, to go to school because of bullying.

- The above information is from the NSPCC's campaign *Cruelty to children must stop. FULL STOP.* Details are on their web site at www.nspcc.org.uk

© NSPCC 2000

---

court in order to remove the child from home.

Children's Hearings

The Reporter to the Children's Panel will be informed if there are concerns that a child is being abused. The Reporter will investigate and decide what action should be taken. He can decide to take no action, or can arrange support for the family on a voluntary basis. If the Reporter thinks it necessary he may refer the child to a Children's Hearing.

The Children's Hearing is made up of ordinary members of the public who have special training. They are appointed to a local 'children's panel'. The hearing's task is to decide what action to take for the child's best interests. The hearing may decide that a child can stay at home but with compulsory supervision from a social worker or the hearing may decide that the child has to live with someone else. The Children's Hearing System is particular to Scotland.

Why do people abuse children?

Much research has been carried out

---

into the situations and background factors which place a child at greater risk of abuse.

Certain factors seem to increase a child's chance of being abused. For example, family stress; perhaps because of financial problems, the parents isolated and having no support. Children with special needs bring extra strain to families. Parenting is a very difficult job and many parents find it hard to cope.

However, it is important to realise that many children living in the most difficult circumstances never experience abuse. While children from 'good' homes can suffer from severe abuse.

Where to find help

If you are a child and are being abused or you know a victim of abuse, talk to an adult you can trust, or you can also ring ChildLine.

Talk to an adult

If you are unable to talk to your parents you can talk to another adult you trust, for example, a teacher, youth club leader, your gran, your minister. You could also contact the social work department or police directly.

ChildLine Helpline – Telephone 0800 1111

A call to ChildLine is free at any time of the day or night. ChildLine deal with any kind of problem, including abuse. If you don't want to phone you can write to them at Freepost 1111, London N1 0BR. You do not need a stamp.

ParentLine Scotland – Freephone 0808 800 2222

If you are a parent or carer and would like to talk things through, call our free helpline ParentLine Scotland. We will listen and help you work out what you need to do and what support is available.

References
1 Waterhouse. L, Dobash. R, and Carnie. J *Child Sexual Abusers* (1994) The Scottish Office
2 *Childhood Matters*, The National Commission into the Prevention of Child Abuse, 1996, Volume 1, London HMSO
3 As above

© *Children 1st*

1m children 'have suffered abuse inside the family'

By Michael Clarke, Home Affairs Correspondent

Almost one million children in Britain have been physically or sexually abused by someone in their family at some point in their lives, the NSPCC claims in a report today.

Experts warned last night, however, that all surveys claiming to show the extent of the problem should be treated with caution.

The society is using its report on abuse to demand a network of highly-paid 'children's commissioners' funded by the taxpayer to 'represent children's interests'.

According to its study of 3,000 young adults, seven per cent said they had suffered 'serious physical abuse' at the hands of a parent or carer.

The nature of the attacks ranged from being hit with a fist or weapon to being beaten up or burned and scalded.

Just over one in 20 said they had been 'seriously physically neglected' at home, including being left without food or being forced to fend for themselves because their parents were drunk or on drugs.

Four per cent told researchers they had suffered sexual abuse within the family, with girls three times as likely as boys to be victims.

An older brother or stepbrother was more often the attacker – blamed in 19 per cent of cases – than a father, accused by 14 per cent.

The study – published to coincide with United Nations' Children's Rights Day – found that poor parents were most likely to abuse their children.

Those in semi-skilled or unskilled jobs were three times as likely as professional people to hit their children.

And the children of professionals were ten times less likely to suffer serious neglect.

Women were said to be more likely to attack their children than men, with mothers responsible for 52 per cent of attacks, and fathers for 45 per cent.

But overall, 92 per cent of those interviewed for the study said they came from a 'warm and loving family background'.

> **Women were said to be more likely to attack their children than men, with mothers responsible for 52 per cent of attacks, and fathers for 45 per cent**

NSPCC chief executive Mary Marsh said the survey showed the need for a network of 'powerful and independent children's commissioners'. The first such £70,000-a-year post has been established in Wales as a result of the Waterhouse inquiry into child abuse in children's homes in the principality.

The key findings . . .

- 7% of children had suffered 'serious physical abuse' from a parent or carer.
- More than one in 20 had been 'seriously physically neglected' at home.
- 4% had suffered sexual abuse in their family.
- Victims of incest were more likely to have been attacked by a brother or stepbrother than their father.
- Children of professionals were 10 times less likely to suffer serious neglect.
- Mothers are 'more likely to attack their children than fathers.

The NSPCC has already criticised the job description set down by the Welsh Assembly as too limited.

The figures in the report are massively lower than those produced in a controversial study four years ago by a commission set up by the same charity and chaired by the present Attorney General, Lord Williams of Mostyn QC.

That claimed one million children a year are abused – a conclusion which was roundly condemned when it emerged that the total included anyone suffering 'emotional abuse', which included allowing them to feel unloved.

The NSPCC study distinguishes between actual physical and sexual abuse and 'mental cruelty'. It makes it clear that physical abuse is much more widespread than incest, despite the much greater attention given to sexual abuse in families.

It fails to distinguish between abuse by stepfathers and stepbrothers and attacks by natural relations, despite the fact that other research has shown most sexual abuse within the family is not carried out by blood relations.

David Marsland, professor of sociology at Brunel University, said: 'It is very important to distinguish between the two, because the truth is most sexual abuse in the family is actually by a stepfather or mother's boyfriend, or by his sons, rather than the real father.'

Another expert warned that the figures could be inflated by 'false memory syndrome' – where adults make up allegations about suffering sex abuse as children.

Yvonne Stayt of Concern for Family and Womanhood, said: 'The thing that I am always concerned about regarding the abuse of children is children who have false memories. I'm sure that abuse does go on, but I'm sceptical about how much.'

© The Daily Mail
November, 2000

Child abuse

Information from ChildLine

What is child abuse?

Although growing up can be difficult, most children and young people receive the love and care they need to develop into healthy, happy young adults. But some children are hurt, neglected and used by adults or other children. Younger children may not be aware that what is happening to them is abuse. Abuse can mean different things to different children, and can happen once or many times.

Physical abuse is . . .

. . . when children are hurt or injured by parents or other people. Hitting, kicking, beating with objects, throwing and shaking are all physical abuse, and can cause pain, cuts, bruising, broken bones and sometimes even death.

Sexual abuse is . . .

. . . when children are forced or persuaded into sexual acts or situations by others. Children might be encouraged to look at pornography, be harassed by sexual suggestions or comments, be touched sexually or forced to have sex.

Emotional abuse is . . .

. . . when children are not given love, approval or acceptance. They may be constantly criticised, blamed, sworn and shouted at, told that other people are better than they are and rejected by those they look to for affection.

Neglect is . . .

. . . when parents or others looking after children do not provide them with proper food, warmth, shelter, clothing, care and protection.

Who abuses children?

It is not just strangers who abuse children. 95% of children calling ChildLine about sexual and physical abuse know the abuser. Abusers include parents, uncles, aunts, grandparents, teachers, family friends, and brothers and sisters. The

majority of abusers are men. They come from all classes, professions and backgrounds. Some women do abuse children, as do young people.

How common is child abuse?

In 1999/2000, 10,036 children and young people (7,388 girls and 2,648 boys) talked to ChildLine about sexual abuse and 14,281 about physical abuse (7,965 girls and 5,316 boys). Most children calling about abuse were between 10 and 14 years old. Children often don't tell about abuse because they have been threatened into keeping silent or made to feel ashamed and guilty.

They may be afraid of what will happen to their family, or that no one will believe them. It is difficult to say exactly how many children are sexually abused. A recent study[1] estimated between 5% and 20% of women and 2%-7% of men had experienced sexual abuse.

> *'I haven't been to school for two days because I'm afraid that people will see the bruises on my arms in PE.'*
>
> *'I thought for a long time that what was happening was okay because Dad said it was a game that all fathers played with their sons, a secret game that only the men knew about.'*
>
> *'I'm in care and I'm always being moved between foster homes. I feel unloved and unsettled.'*
>
> *'My mum and dad both have drinking problems. Sometimes there's nothing to eat in the house. And I'm often left alone to look after my brothers and sisters.'*

What are the effects of child abuse?

Child abuse sometimes causes physical injury, and often leaves emotional scars. People who have grown up being abused can feel worthless, unlovable, betrayed, powerless, confused, frightened and mistrustful of others. They might feel, wrongly, that the abuse is their fault. Talking to somebody who can be trusted can help children to feel better.

Things children should know if they are worried about child abuse

- Children have a right to be safe.
- Children are not to blame for being abused – the person hurting them is the one who has done wrong.
- Children shouldn't feel they have to deal with abuse on their own.
- Children should tell a person they can trust, such as a parent, teacher, relative or friend, if they are being abused in any way, even if they are worried about what might happen next.
- It is okay for children not to keep secrets about being abused.
- Children may not be believed when they talk about abuse. This does not mean they are lying. They should try to find someone who will believe them, or phone ChildLine.

What happens if a child tells someone about being abused?

Children often find it hard to tell an adult about the abuse. They sometimes feel that it is their fault, and they are also are worried about the consequences of telling – that they will be taken from their homes, or that the family will be broken up, or that their parents will get into trouble. They may, however, feel able to talk to another member of their family, for example, an aunt or grandparent. Often families can protect and help children themselves. Children may choose to speak to someone outside their family, for example, a teacher or youth club leader. Many also ring ChildLine.

Under our law, some adults, like teachers, must pass on the information to the police or social services. If a child phones ChildLine to talk about being abused, the counsellor does not have to tell anyone else. Nothing is passed on to the police or social services unless the child wants to take that step or is in serious danger.

There are laws to help protect children and to bring perpetrators to justice. The laws are different in Scotland and Northern Ireland, but they work in the same way. The most important laws are the Children Act 1989 (England and Wales), the Children (Scotland) Act 1995 and the Children (Northern Ireland) Order 1995. These Acts describe what should happen if a child tells about being abused, or is in danger of suffering 'significant harm'.

In law, the local authority has a duty to make enquiries about any allegation of abuse. This means that a social worker may come to talk to the child and the parents, and try to find out the facts, and decide whether the child is in any danger of abuse or neglect. Many investigations go no further than this, but sometimes, social workers decide that they need to have a child protection conference.

A child protection conference

is called by the local authority to talk about their worries about the child, and to decide what to do next. Usually, many people from the child's life are invited – teachers, doctors, health visitors, playworkers, as well as the police and social workers. The child and their family may also be invited.

If the conference decides that the child is at risk of significant harm, they may decide to put his or her name on the child protection register. Social Services departments hold a central register in their area of all children considered to be at risk of abuse, and for whom there is a child protection plan. The conference can decide to help the family in caring and looking after the child, or it sometimes decides that the child is at too much risk staying in the family home, and needs to live somewhere else, perhaps with foster parents for a while.

The law can also make the person who is believed to be the abuser leave the family home, rather than the child. The police

have to go to court to get agreement and it is only for a certain time, but it means that the child can stay in their familiar home, with the other parent and members of their family.

Once a child has made an allegation, the police may also be involved, and the child may be interviewed on video by a member of the police child protection team. The police do this in order to gather evidence to bring the perpetrator to court, and the child may go to court to give evidence when the case is heard.

This can be a harrowing time for children, but with a loving family and counselling or therapeutic help when they need it, there is every hope and chance that they will get better.

Can sex offenders be prevented from abusing again?

If someone abuses a child, they are committing a criminal offence, and can be prosecuted and imprisoned. In prison, some abusers will be offered treatment. There is much discussion about whether treatment of abusers works – in some cases, it doesn't, but in other cases treatment can help offenders control their behaviour. When an offender leaves prison, he now has to register his address with the local police, so that his where-abouts can be monitored. Courts can also prohibit an offender from going to specific places, for example, playgrounds or schools.

Although these measures help police keep track of known sex offenders, they do not remove the need for parents, children and the public to all take responsibility for protecting children. Giving children information and confidence is the basis of preventing abuse.

Reference
1   Kelly, Regan, Burton, Child and Woman Abuse Studies Unit. (1991) An exploratory study of the pre-valence of sexual abuse in a sample of 16-21 year olds. London: University of North London

How does ChildLine help?

Children who have been abused can feel very confused and scared about what has happened, and unsure about what to do. It can take a lot of courage to start talking about abuse, but talking to a counsellor at ChildLine can help children feel less lonely and isolated, feel better about themselves, feel more confident and able to think about ways of seeking help.

ChildLine has a policy of confidentiality. ChildLine counsellors will not pass on any information about the child to any other agency, and all the conversations between the child and ChildLine remain private.

ChildLine will only break confidentiality against the wishes of the child, if there is a danger to the child's life. Sometimes, after talking to a counsellor, a child may wish ChildLine to talk on his or her behalf to an adult in their lives, for example, a teacher or family friend. ChildLine will do so, and will help the child to talk directly to that trusted adult. Counsellors will also give the child information and advice about speaking to the police and social services, and, if the child decides to do so, will support the child through that process.

ChildLine is free and available 24 hours a day, seven days a week.
ChildLine
Freephone: 0800 1111 or
Freepost 1111, London N1 0BR or
ChildLine Minicom: 0800 400 222
Mon – Fri, 9.30am – 9.30pm
Sat – Sun, 9.30am – 8.00pm

ChildLine reports

MacLeod, M (1997) *Child protection – everybody's business* (£5 + 50p p&p) London: ChildLine/ Community Care

MacLeod, M (1996) *Talking with children about child abuse* (£5 + 50p p&p) London: ChildLine.

Keep, G (1996) *Going to court: child witnesses in their own words* (£3 + 50p p&p) London: ChildLine

Who are the abusers?

Information from Scottish Women's Aid

Child sexual abuse is a crime most commonly committed by men against both girls and boys. The vast majority of abuse is committed by men – 95% of abusers are male. Women are between two and three times more likely to have experienced sexual abuse than men.

It is essential to realise that abuse is a gender issue, and is a result of the power imbalance within our society. At the same time it is vital to believe and support all survivors of sexual abuse which can be perpetrated by men, women, peers, and groups of people.

Children are more likely to be abused by someone they know and trust or by someone in authority than by a stranger. Abusers include: adults, parents, trusted adults/authority figures, other children, relatives, babysitters, neighbours, etc.

Children can be sexually abused at any age, from infancy to adolescence.

The sexual abuse of children occurs within every neighbourhood, class, racial background.

Indicators of sexual abuse
Children show distress in many ways, emotionally and physically, and these could be possible indicators of abuse – emotional and physical as well as sexual:
- Destructive behaviour to themselves or others
- Withdrawn attitude (not playing or lack of trust), very passive
- Clinging, touching, crying but not saying what's wrong
- Wanting to please, looking for approval
- Sexually overt behaviour
- Eating problems
- Disruptive behaviour, violence, bullying, destructive, criminal behaviour
- Not wanting to do PE at school, not wanting to undress
- Not wanting to go home/parents to go out, running away
- Self mutilating
- Bed wetting, pain/fear when going to the toilet
- Illness
- Seeking attention
- Mood swings, depression
- Tiredness, not sleeping
- Suicide attempts
- Strange or particular fears
Survivors are affected by their individual experiences in different ways, and children may show any combination of the above or none at all.

- The above information is an extract from *Children – Equality and Respect*, produced by Scottish Women's Aid. See page 41 for their address details.

Signs and symptoms

Information from Kidscape

Although these signs do not necessarily indicate that a child has been abused, they may help adults recognise that something is wrong. The possibility of abuse should be investigated if a child shows a number of these symptoms, or any of them to a marked degree:

Sexual abuse
- Being overly affectionate or knowledgeable in a sexual way inappropriate to the child's age.
- Medical problems such as chronic itching, pain in the genitals, venereal diseases.
- Other extreme reactions, such as depression, self-mutilation, suicide attempts, running away, overdoses, anorexia.
- Personality changes such as becoming insecure or clinging.
- Regressing to younger behaviour patterns such as thumb sucking or bringing out discarded cuddly toys.
- Sudden loss of appetite or compulsive eating.
- Being isolated or withdrawn.
- Inability to concentrate.
- Lack of trust or fear of someone they know well, such as not wanting to be alone with a babysitter or child minder.
- Starting to wet again, day or night/nightmares.
- Become worried about clothing being removed.
- Suddenly drawing sexually explicit pictures.
- Trying to be 'ultra-good' or perfect; overreacting to criticism.

Physical abuse
- Unexplained recurrent injuries or burns.
- Improbable excuses or refusal to explain injuries.
- Wearing clothes to cover injuries, even in hot weather.
- Refusal to undress for gym.
- Bald patches.
- Chronic running away.
- Fear of medical help or examination.
- Self-destructive tendencies.
- Aggression towards others.
- Fear of physical contact – shrinking back if touched.
- Admitting that they are punished, but the punishment is excessive (such as a child being beaten every night to 'make him study').
- Fear of suspected abuser being contacted.

Emotional abuse
- Physical, mental and emotional development lags.
- Sudden speech disorders.
- Continual self-depreciation ('I'm stupid, ugly, worthless, etc.')
- Overreaction to mistakes.
- Extreme fear of any new situation.
- Inappropriate response to pain ('I deserve this').
- Neurotic behaviour (rocking, hair twisting, self-mutilation).
- Extremes of passivity or aggression.

Neglect
- Constant hunger.
- Poor personal hygiene.
- Constant tiredness.
- Poor state of clothing.
- Emaciation.
- Untreated medical problems.
- No social relationships.
- Compulsive scavenging.
- Destructive tendencies.

Note:
- A child may be subjected to a combination of different kinds of abuse.
- It is also possible that a child may show no outward signs and hide what is happening from everyone.

Suspected abuse
If you suspect that a child is being abused, seek advice from the police or social services. It is preferable that you identify yourself and give details. However, if you feel unsure and would like to discuss the situation,

ring the National Society for the Prevention of Cruelty to Children (NSPCC) Helpline, or the Royal Scottish Society for the Prevention of Cruelty to Children, or the Irish Society for the Prevention of Cruelty to Children. You can speak to these organisations (and the police and social services) anonymously. The numbers are at the end of this article.

Knowing how damaging abuse is to children, it is up to the adults around them to take responsibility for stopping it.

Telling

If a child tells you about abuse:
- Stay calm and be reassuring.
- Find a quiet place to talk.
- Believe in what you are being told.
- Listen, but do not press for information.
- Say that you are glad that the child told you.
- If it will help the child to cope, say that the abuser has a problem.
- Say that you will do your best to protect and support the child.
- If necessary, seek medical help and contact the police or social services.
- If your child has told another adult, such as a teacher or school nurse, contact them. Their advice may make it easier to help your child.
- Determine if this incident may affect how your child reacts at school. It may be advisable to liaise with your child's teacher, school nurse or headteacher.
- Acknowledge that your child may have angry, sad or even guilty feelings about what happened, but stress that the abuse was not the child's fault. Acknowledge that you will probably need help dealing with your own feelings.
- Seek counselling for yourself and your child through the organisations listed or through your own contacts.

Where to get help

You may consider using the school as a resource, as the staff should have a network of agencies they work with, and be able to give you advice.

You can contact official agencies

Knowing how damaging abuse is to children, it is up to the adults around them to take responsibility for stopping it

---

or self-help groups. If you are concerned about what action may be taken, ask before you proceed.

The following can be contacted through your telephone directory:
- Police
- Social Services
- Samaritans 0345 90 90 90
- National Society for the Prevention of Cruelty to Children (NSPCC) in England, Wales and Northern Ireland freephone 0800 800 500
- Children First 0131 337 8539

- Irish Society for the Prevention of Cruelty to Children (ISPCC) 00 353 742 9744
- ChildLine 0800 1111
- Parentline 0808 800 2222

For a free copy of the leaflet *Why My Child?* which helps parents deal with the sexual abuse of their child, send a large SAE marked 'Why My Child?' with 60p stamp to: Kidscape, 2 Grosvenor Gardens, London SW1W 0DH. Tel: 020 7730 3300. Web site: www.kidscape.org.uk E-mail: info@kidscape.org.uk

Kidscape offers training and literature to parents, children and those who work with them. Kidscape is reliant on donations. Kidscape is a registered charity founded in 1984 with the aim of teaching children, their parents and other concerned adults ways of keeping children safe.

© Reproduced with kind permission from Kidscape

The causes of cruelty

Information from the NSPCC

The NSPCC defines child cruelty as '. . . neglect, physical injury, sexual or emotional abuse inflicted or knowingly not prevented, which causes significant harm or death'.

There's no one theory to explain why children are ill-treated. But research has identified some broader causes:

Individual psychology
The personalities of some people may make it more likely they will harm children.

Interactions between adults and children
Sometimes, adults become over-dominant. This imbalance of power can end in child abuse.

Social factors
Poverty, unemployment and discrimination place intolerable pressures on individuals. This can lead them to harm the children in their care.

Cultural factors
Our society fails to give children their real value. Children are often seen as objects not individuals, so their needs aren't given the priority they deserve.

Welfare and child protection systems have also been criticised. People feel they'll be branded as poor parents if they go to these places for help. In many cases, professionals have failed to spot which children are in real danger of abuse.

- The above information is from the NSPCC's campaign *Cruelty to children must stop. FULL STOP*. Details are on their web site at www.nspcc.org.uk

© NSPCC 2000

When I was a little girl

This week a survey found that 1m British children suffer violence at home. Author Andrea Ashworth, who was abused as a child, is at least glad it's out in the open

When I was a little girl, my mother wore sunglasses a lot of the time – even when it was raining. Under the glasses, her skin would be swollen and sometimes cut. My sisters and I watched each bruise go through its sickening rainbow – scarlet, purple and yellow, green, black and blue – before her face was itself again.

My father had drowned when I was five years old, my little sister three. My mother married a new man, with whom she had a baby, and from that moment we lived in a terrifying, topsy-turvy world. My stepfather would hit us, about the head and in the face, for any reason or no reason at all: a splash of spilled water, a misplaced sock, even the sight of my sister or me reading a book. Occasionally, when he was especially careless, I would be thrown into a concussion. If my mother cried or tried to stop our stepfather from hurting us, he would turn on her. We regularly saw our mother being throttled, punched in the face, hurled against the wall or the floor and threatened with boiling water and knives.

After each explosion, my stepfather would thrust his hand over my face until I gagged. He whispered foul, graphic threats to let me know just what he would do if ever I, the eldest child, opened my mouth to tell. He made me terrified of confiding in my own mother about his private assaults on me. I never dreamed of telling the world what went on behind our stripy green curtains.

At school, my nickname was Smiler. I scooted around the playground, a vivacious child, giving my teachers no cause for concern. Even without my stepfather's threats and the clamp of his hand over my mouth, I would not have dared – back then – to appeal to a teacher or any 'outsider' for help. I put my smile on, over the secrets, and waited for it to be knocked off again when I went home.

By Andrea Ashworth

Why? Why didn't I say a word?

In the first place, although my sisters and I lived in daily terror, it never occurred to me that we could, or even should, expect anything different. Children can be marvellously, but also dangerously, elastic, adapting to adversity, growing to regard it as normal. As I grew up, I began to realise that what went on in my family was not normal but quite horrific. Seeing this, I was struck dumb by a deep sense of shame. Domestic abuse was not, in the 70s and early 80s, something to be discussed in public. I had never even heard of terms such as neglect or abuse, let alone imagined them being applied to my family. Moreover my mother and sisters and I suffered a sense of guilt about what was done to us, as if we deserved it. Like many

The NSPCC's latest survey reveals that child abuse is, as we ought to have known, and cared about, all along, shockingly widespread

victims, we were caught in a web of silence, woven from sticky strands of guilt and fear, desperate hope, shame and, stickiest of all, love.

Just before I left home at the age of 18, I climbed into a tiny aeroplane, took off into the clouds and turned green, going through loop-the-loops and barrel rolls on a sponsored aerobatic flight that helped to raise money for the National Society for the Prevention of Cruelty to Children. I wasn't sure why I was doing it, why I had chosen to support that cause, what that cause was exactly. I puked my insides out on the third loop and came down giggling, feeling drunk. I was still someone behind whose big smile lurked an agonising story.

Suffering in silence, my family and I went through experiences that are, in all ways, unspeakable. This shroud of silence, psychologically suffocating and literally lethal, was – and is – one of the most insidious aspects of domestic abuse. Especially for children whose voices are small. The NSPCC's latest survey reveals that child abuse is, as we ought to have known, and cared about, all along, shockingly widespread. Children desperately need to be rescued from daily torment and from futures in which they will recycle mental, physical and sexual abuse, painfully reliving it, and passing it on.

Thanks to the passionate and messy work of charities like the NSPCC, thanks to a salutary swing in the media's searchlights, thanks to our efforts to look at and understand ourselves as a society, stories like mine are no longer so shamefully suppressed. Families do not have to fester in secret. Smashing the silence is a crucial first step in smashing a cycle that we have lived with too quietly, too long.

• *Once in a House on Fire* is published in paperback by Picador at £6.99.

Survey reveals widespread child abuse

By John Carvel

More sexual abuse of children is perpetrated by siblings than by fathers or step-fathers and violence towards children is more likely to come from mothers than fathers, according to a survey for the National Society for the Prevention of Cruelty to Children.

The charity, which last night demanded urgent government response to its findings, published the most comprehensive survey so far of child abuse in the UK, showing 6% suffered serious physical neglect, 6% were emotionally maltreated and 1% were sexually abused by a parent.

Mary Marsh, the charity's director, called on the government to rethink its opposition to the appointment of children's commissioners for England, Scotland and Northern Ireland.

'The appointment of such watchdogs, as is being advanced in Wales and across Europe, must be the government's first response to this report.'

The charity's findings come from a UK-wide survey of the childhood experiences of 2,869 young people aged 18-24 by the research company BMRB International.

By asking a large representative sample of young adults to give their recollections confidentially on computer terminals, the charity thinks it obtained the most accurate picture so far of the extent of abuse. It says it would have been ethically wrong and difficult to survey children directly.

According to the findings, published today on UN Children's Rights Day, one in 14 suffered serious physical abuse at the hands of parents or carers, including being hit with a fist or implement, beaten up, or burned and scalded on purpose.

That proportion is equivalent to nearly 1m of the children in Britain today. The NSPCC said 49% of the victims were treated violently by their mother, 40% by their father and 8% by a step-parent.

One in 12 suffered bullying and discrimination regularly and more than four in 10 experienced it at some point. In the first polling research into the prevalence of emotional maltreatment, the charity found 6% experienced multiple attacks on their self-esteem, including terrorising, humiliation, withdrawal of affection and harming of possessions or pets. Girls were twice as likely as boys to suffer from this type of cruelty.

> 'Some young people interviewed in this research suffered serious forms of abuse during their formative years, often on a regular basis and often in silence.'

One in 10 – mostly girls – have been forced into sex acts under the age of 16 and involving people known to them. In 43% of cases, the perpetrator was a brother or step-brother, compared with 19% saying a stepfather and 14% naming their father.

The survey found more than nine in 10 young people said they grew up in a loving family, but one in four said there were childhood events that they found difficult to talk about.

Ms Marsh said: 'For many young people, serious stresses and unhappiness cast a dark shadow over what should have been an otherwise happy childhood.

'Some young people interviewed in this research suffered serious forms of abuse during their formative years, often on a regular basis and often in silence. For many, the damage done will last long into adulthood.'

She repeated the charity's call for independent commissioners to protect children, similar to the statutory bodies for women, ethnic minorities and disabled people. This was Labour policy in its 1992 election manifesto, but was dropped in 1997.

A Department of Health spokesman said: 'Any type of child abuse is unacceptable and the government has already taken steps to tackle this. This includes a national care standards commission by April 2002 with 70 officers around the country.

'It will have a national director for vulnerable children who will understand the new standards for those in care or at risk of abuse.'

But David Hinchliffe, Labour chairman of the Commons health committee, said: 'The time is ripe for the government to follow the example of other European countries by introducing an independent children's rights commissioner... There are now no excuses for putting off such a move.'

Julian Brazier, president of the Conservative Family Campaign, said: 'I'm very much in support of the campaign for a children's commissioner. I strongly believe that politicians and the public must unite to help the NSPCC rid society of cruelty to children.'

Child protection

Information from NCH Action for Children

Children on child protection registers

Children who are considered to be suffering from or likely to suffer significant harm and for whom there is a child protection plan have their names registered on a central child protection register held by each local social services department in the UK. Registration takes place following a child protection case conference, at which professionals make decisions about whether the level of risk to the child is sufficient for the child's name to be placed on the register. If the child is registered, an inter-agency child protection plan is drawn up and agreed between the professionals involved with the child and his or her family.

There are four main categories of child abuse under which a child's name can be registered: neglect, physical abuse, sexual abuse and emotional abuse. Where registration is required or necessary, a child is usually registered under one main category of abuse but may be registered under more.

On 31 March 1999 there were a total of 31,900 children on child protection registers in England, 1% more than the previous year. This represents a rate of 28 children per 10,000 in the population aged under 18. The numbers on registers reached 45,000 in 1991 but then fell sharply over the next two years. Since then the numbers have been relatively stable.

Of the 31,900 children on child protection registers, 16,000 (51%) were boys and 15,600 (49%) were girls.

At 31 March 1999 there were 3,000 children under one year of age, 9% of the total, a proportion which has risen slowly over the previous decade. At the other end of the age range 600 or 2% were aged 16 and over; this number has been falling steadily.

Children aged under one had the highest registration rate (71 per

10,000 children in that age group). The rate was lower for the age group one to four (35) and continues to decline up the age range, falling to four for children aged over 15. For numbers on the register the pattern was similar although the differences between age groups were less marked.

Re-registrations to child protection registers in England

Of the 30,100 registrations in the year ending 31 March 1999 it is estimated that 4,600 (15%) were re-registrations, i.e. children who had been on the register previously. This represents a sharp fall from the figure of 19% a year earlier, after having risen steadily since 1992 when figures were first collected.

In November 1998 the Department of Health established 're-registrations to the child protection register' as an indicator of children's social services under the Quality

Protects programme. The Department has also set the related National Priorities Guidance target to: 'reduce by 10% by 2002, the proportion of children who are re-registered on the child protection register, from a baseline for the year ending March 1997'. This target would require a reduction from the 1996-97 figure of 19.4% to 17.2% by 2001-02.

Source: *Children and Young People on Child Protection Registers – Year ending 31 March 1999, England.* Department of Health, 1999.

Length of time on the register in England

Information was collected about the time that children who were de-registered had spent on the register. During the year ending 31 March 1999, it is estimated that about 7,600 children (25%) had been on the register under six months, and 4,200 (14%) had been on the register for two years or more. The equivalent percentages a year earlier were 26% and 13% respectively. The percentage of children leaving the register who had been on it for more than two years fell between 1994 and 1996 but has now levelled off. This measure has also been established as an indicator of children's social

services under the Quality Protects programme and should be considered alongside the indicator of re-registrations described above.

Similar patterns are seen for both registrations and numbers. Neglect is the most commonly used category, being used for 42% of children registered during 1998-99. This proportion has risen steadily since 1995, when 30% of registrations involved neglect. The number of cases for which emotional abuse has been recorded has also risen over the same period. In contrast, the use of physical injury and emotional abuse categories has steadily fallen.

During 1998-99 girls had a higher rate of registration because of a risk of sexual abuse than boys. For sexual abuse the rate of registration was six per 10,000 girls and four per 10,000 boys in the population. This abuse category accounted for 23% of registrations for girls during the year and 16% of registrations for boys. Boys were more likely to be placed on the register because of a risk of physical injury than girls. For boys, 33% of registrations were in connection with physical injury compared with 30% for girls.

Source: *Children and Young People on Child Protection Registers – Year ending 31 March 1999, England*. Department of Health, 1999.

Looked after children on the register in England

At 31 March 1999, 7,900 children (25% of those on the register) in England were looked after by local authorities. This figure represents 15% of all children looked after at that date.

Sixty-four per cent of these looked after children were subject to care orders with most of the remainder looked after under voluntary agreements. Two-thirds were accommodated in foster placements, a proportion similar to that for all looked after children, with a further 8% in children's homes and 18% placed with parents.

Source: *Children and Young People on Child Protection Registers – Year ending 31 March 1999, England*. Department of Health, 1999.

Children and young people on child protection registers in Wales

On 31 March 1998 there were 2,473 children on child protection registers in Wales, an increase of 448 on the previous year and representing a rate of 37 per 10,000 children aged under 18. The highest rates were in the 1-4 years age group for girls and the under one year age group for boys; for the older age groups the rate decreased as the age increased. The overall rates on the register were higher for girls than boys. Compared to 1992, a lower proportion of children on the registers were in the 5-9 years and 16-17 years age groups.

There were 2,025 registrations and 2,039 de-registrations. Thirty-one per cent of the registrations were recorded in the neglect (only) category, 26% under physical abuse (only), 11% under sexual abuse (only) and 22% under emotional abuse.

Physical abuse was involved in 34% of cases registered and sexual abuse was involved in 15% of cases. As in England, neglect (only) was the largest category for both boys and girls. The trend since 1994 has been a fall in the proportion of cases categorised as sexual abuse (only), with considerable increases in those recorded under emotional abuse and neglect.

Source: *Child Protection Register: Statistics for Wales 1998*. Welsh Office, 1999.

• The above information is an extract from *NCH Factfile 2001*, ISBN 0 900984 70 8. £7.50. Factfile is NCH's annual compendium of key facts and statistics about Britain's children.

© NCH Action for Children

Child protection

Numbers on child protection registers in England
Children and young people on child protection registers in England at 31 March 1999, by age and gender

| | Age at 31 March 1999 | | | | | |
	All ages	Under 1	1-4	5-9	10-15	16+
Numbers[1]						
All children[2]	31,900	3,000	9,700	9,700	8,600	600
Boys	16,000	1,500	5,000	4,200	300	
Girls	15,600	1,500	4,700	4,700	4,400	400
Rates[3]						
All children	28	50	39	30	23	5
Boys	28	50	39	30	22	4
Girls	28	50	39	29	24	6

1 Figures may not add due to rounding
2 The 'All Ages, all children' figures include 300 unborn children.
3 Rates are per 10,000 population in each age and gender group

Registrations to child protection registers in England
Registrations to and de-registrations from child protection registers by gender, at 31 March 1999, England.

	All children[1]	Boys	Girls
Registrations	30,100	14,700	14,600
De-registrations	29,600	14,900	14,700

1 The 'All children' figures include unborn children.

Categories of abuse: England
Registrations to child protection registers by category of abuse in England, numbers and percentages

Category of abuse	On the register	
	1998	1999
Neglect	13,000	13,900
Physical injury	9,900	9,100
Sexual abuse	6,700	6,600
Emotional abuse	5,200	5,400
No category available	200	200

Percentages		
Neglect	41%	44%
Physical injury	31%	29%
Sexual abuse	21%	21%
Emotional abuse	16%	17%
No category available	1%	1%

Source: Children and Young People on Child Protection Registers – Year Ending 31 March 1999 – England, Department of Health, 1999. Crown Copyright

Child maltreatment in the UK

A study of the prevalence of child abuse and neglect

Summary of research findings

Child Maltreatment in the United Kingdom is the most authoritative survey of child maltreatment, abuse and neglect yet undertaken in the UK. The study is based on 'random-probability' interviews with 2,869 young people aged 18-24 conducted by survey research company BMRB International between September 1998 and February 1999.

More than nine out of ten young people interviewed said they grew up in warm and loving families. But one in three respondents also reported that there was sometimes 'a lot of stress' in their families. The same proportion reported financial pressures and worries. More than a quarter said 'there are things that happened in my childhood that I find hard to talk about'.

Children from all social backgrounds suffer abuse and maltreatment. But the survey found strong links between serious physical abuse or neglect and the current socio-economic grade of the respondent, reflecting both aspects of their social background and the damaging effect that adverse childhood experience has on educational and other life chances.

Physical violence against children in the UK is primarily a family affair. Seven per cent of the young people suffered serious physical abuse at the hands of parents and carers, including being hit with a fist or an implement, beaten up, burned and scalded. Mothers were as likely as fathers to physically abuse their children.

The young people reported that most parents used physical punishment rarely and lightly, but a minority used it regularly and severely. Parents who smacked their children regularly often caused bruising, pain or soreness lasting at least until next day – it seemed that the frequent users of physical punishment were also likely to be the most severe users.

NSPCC
Cruelty to children must stop. FULL STOP.

Six per cent of respondents suffered serious absence of physical care at home, including regularly being left without food as a young child, not being looked after or taken to the doctor when ill, or being left to fend for themselves because parents were absent or had drug or alcohol problems.

There had also been serious absence of supervision of some respondents, with one per cent allowed to stay at home alone overnight when they were under 10 and four per cent allowed out overnight with their whereabouts unknown when they were under 14.

Emotional abuse is one of the most hidden and often under-estimated forms of child maltreatment. The study found that almost six per cent of respondents had suffered multiple attacks on their well-being within their families. These included, among others, living with frequent violence between their parents, having treasured possessions deliberately destroyed by parents, being regularly humiliated, or being told that their parents wished them dead or never born.

Sexual abuse of children within the family is less common. One per cent of young people were sexually assaulted by a parent or carer. Three per cent of the young people suffered sexual abuse by another relative, ranging from penetrative or oral sex to taking pornographic photographs of them. A wide range of – mainly male – relatives were involved, most often brothers or stepbrothers. Girls were far more likely than boys to experience all forms of sexual abuse.

Sexual violence is more likely to take place outside the family than within it. One in ten young people had experienced penetrative sex, oral sex or attempts at these against their will by people unrelated to them. Nearly all were people known to the child, most commonly 'boyfriends', friends of brothers or sisters, or fellow students.

Many of those who experienced coercive sex acts reported the use of physical force or threat. Girls were far more likely than boys to have experienced coercive sexual activity.

Almost one in three young people had never told anyone about their unwanted sexual experiences, and only just over a quarter had sought help at the time.

The only category of unwanted sexual activity experienced to any great extent from strangers (usually men) was indecent exposure. But two per cent of the young people reported sexual abuse involving physical contact by a stranger or someone recently met.

The most common source of distress and misery to children is bullying and discrimination by other young people. 43 per cent of the young people were bullied or discriminated against by other children, and eight per cent said this happened regularly over years. They were bullied mostly because of personal characteristics such as size, dress, race or manner of speech. Name-calling, insults and verbal abuse were most common but 14 to 15 per cent were physically attacked, and many young people also experienced having their property stolen or damaged. The overwhelming number of bullying incidents took place at school.

Conclusion

Families are the primary source of love and nurturing for nearly all children. But significant minorities of children are confronted – either occasionally or regularly – by stresses, problems and abusive behaviour with which they should not have to cope.

For many children too, the wider world of school, friends and community is one which is fraught with the threats of bullying, discrimination and – particularly for girls – sexual harassment and violence.

This study underlines the need for children's voices to be heard by the people who can help them. Children need the self-confidence to speak out and someone they trust and in whom they can confide.

Large numbers of children find it too difficult to talk about the abuse and difficulties which they face in their lives. If they do tell someone, it is very unlikely to be a professional concerned with their care. In this way, distressing and harmful childhood experiences can remain hidden for many years.

In terms of severity and frequency, there are different levels of child maltreatment. When children at risk of significant harm are identified, children's services must act quickly and decisively to protect them. And firm action against carers may be appropriate when a child has suffered serious abuse or neglect.

However, not all cruelty to children is planned or intended to cause harm. Our approach to child protection must be a sophisticated one, geared up for preventing child abuse and neglect.

Although children from all social backgrounds can suffer maltreatment, the study found strong links between serious physical abuse or neglect and socio-economic grade. This indicates that children in families facing poverty and social exclusion are particularly vulnerable.

If we are serious about reducing the incidence of child cruelty, we must give more support to those families pushed to the limits by extreme stress, medical conditions or socio-economic pressures.

This report presents a challenge to society in general, and professionals and policy-makers in particular, to create the conditions whereby no child has to worry about going hungry or being assaulted in the family home.

It also challenges us to rethink the ways we support families in the UK and care for children both inside and outside the family setting. Most child abuse goes unreported or undetected. We need to find ways to reach its many hidden victims.

We know that cruelty to children can be brought to a full stop, if the will to do so exists.

• The above information is an extract from the NSPCC publication *Child maltreatment in the UK*. See page 41 for their address details.

© *NSPCC*

The extent of violence involving children

Children are far more often victims of violence than perpetrators of violence, and certain groups of children, including disabled children and some ethnic groups, are particularly at risk. One of the most disturbing social statistics is that the risk of homicide for babies under the age of one is almost four times as great as for any other age group. There is increasing knowledge of and sensitivity to violence to children – in particular to sexual abuse and to bullying and other violence in institutions; it is not possible to tell whether the incidence of these forms of violence has increased or become more visible. There are problems about building any accurate picture of violence to children within families, but the most recent UK research shows that a substantial minority of children suffer severe physical punishment; most children are hit by their parents, up to a third of younger children more than once a week.

Only a very small proportion of children – mostly male but with an increasing minority of young women – get involved in committing violent offences. Very roughly, four per 1,000 young people aged between 10 and 18 are cautioned or convicted for offences involving violence against the person.

In terms of trends it appears that children's involvement in some but not all crimes of violence in the UK has increased over the last decade. But in comparison with the USA, overall levels of interpersonal violence in the UK are very low, and there is recent evidence that in comparison with some European countries, levels of self-reported violence by children in the UK are also low.

• The above information is an extract from *Children and Violence*, a summary of a report produced by the Calouste Gulbenkian Foundation. The book of the same name is available from Turnaround Publisher Services Ltd. Tel. 020 8829 3000; e-mail orders@turnaround-uk.com Alternatively visit the foundation's web site at www.gulbenkian.org.uk

© *Calouste Gulbenkian Foundation*

No child's play

**Amid growing awareness of sexual abuse between siblings,
Linda Jackson reports on projects making a difference**

Sarah was looking forward to seeing her two young children after a hard day's work at the office. But her joy at spending the evening with them turned to dismay when she discovered that her four-year-old daughter, Sally, had been sexually abused. Equally shocking was the revelation that the abuser was her six-year-old son, Nigel. His behaviour emerged only when Sally told her mother she didn't like playing doctors any more. Asked why, she replied: 'I don't like it when Nigel examines me and gives me operations.'

Sadly, Nigel and his sister's case is far from unique. Recent research shows that sexual abuse and inappropriate sexual behaviour between young siblings is far more common than abuse by other family members such as fathers and stepfathers. What is new is that local authorities and child protection charities are starting to concentrate on this area of abuse after more than a decade when adult men have been cast as the villains.

In Nigel's case, an investigation by social services found that his mother's previous partner had often been violent towards the whole family and had forced Sarah into sexual behaviour in front of the children.

The young boy was assessed and his mother agreed to a pioneering programme of work with Warwickshire's 'sexualised inappropriate behaviour service' (Sibs). Work took place over the next six months with the family. This involved counselling and help with parent skills for the mother, and joint play work with the children to help them talk through their experience and develop appropriate behaviour.

That was 18 months ago. Social services support for the family has now been withdrawn. But Warwickshire social services department is still running Sibs – one of the few local authorities specialising in this area – amid growing recognition that sexual abuse of children by children is one of the most common forms of sexual abuse.

Only last month, a report by the NSPCC challenged the widespread belief that fathers are chiefly responsible for sexual abuse of children. A survey of the childhood experiences of 2,869 young people aged 18-24 found that abuse by brothers or stepbrothers was twice as common as that by a father or stepfather.

A survey of the childhood experiences of 2,869 young people aged 18-24 found that abuse by brothers or stepbrothers was twice as common as that by a father or stepfather.

The findings were splashed across the newspapers, and commentators predicted that the findings would trigger a major change in approach to sexual abuse in the family. But probation officers and social workers say awareness of sibling abuse has been growing for years. Interviews with adult sex offenders have revealed a cycle of abuse, with offenders starting their abuse in their early teens after being the victim of sexual or physical assaults. However, experts admit it is only now that therapeutic work with young abusers is being offered as a specialist service.

Driven by a real desire to break this predatory pattern of abuse, Andrew Durham, a senior social worker, set up the project in Warwickshire. What began as a joint health and social services initiative has developed into a permanent specialist assessment and treatment service that has been hailed by the government's social services inspectorate as an example of good practice.

Figures show the high demand for the service, which works sympathetically with young people to retrain and redirect their sexual behaviour. Between 1998 and 1999, Sibs dealt with 62 cases of sexually inappropriate behaviour and child sexual abuse – ranging from over-sexualised five-year-olds, to sexually abusive 11-year-olds and 14-year-old rapists. Three in four referrals were for children aged 10 and over. Ninety per cent of children referred to the project were boys. Most of the victims were female.

The story of Nigel and Sally, in which Nigel tried to simulate sexual intercourse, is drawn from actual cases worked on by Sibs. Most children referred to the project are older. One typical case involved two families where a young teenage boy from one family was found playing 'sexual' games with a younger boy and girl from another. Interviews revealed the teenager had been using his father's collection of pornography and was being bullied at school. He was given a police caution following his family's agreement to work with Sibs – work which took place over 12 months. The children in the other family were also offered help and support from the local social services children's team.

The age of the children referred for help may vary – but most share a vulnerability, according to Mr Durham, who has received an advanced award in social work in recognition of his work on the project. 'Young people who abuse often have very difficult problems in their lives, which they are unable to deal with in the ways most people do,' he says. 'They often have experiences of being powerless, of being put down. They want to feel more powerful. For boys, in a distorted way, it reinforces their feelings of being male.'

An analysis of cases seen in 1998 shows that 80% of children had family problems. Of these, 54% had been sexually abused, 45% were in care, 28% were physically abused and 42% were emotionally abused. More than half (52%) had problems at school.

Cases are referred to Sibs through the police, social services or schools. An assessment is made of the child or young person and of their willingness to work with the project. An assessment of the family is also made and the social worker makes every effort to work with the parents, who may be angry or in denial. Part of the Sibs work involves setting up a network of people, including the family, to support the young person. They are given practical guidelines to help prevent opportunities where the young person might abuse again. If the young person agrees to work with Sibs, a sexual history is taken. Boys who may want a macho image are taught to be assertive, rather than aggressive.

A similar approach is taken in Oxfordshire, where the Oxfordshire young abusers' project (Oxyap) has been treating young people for the past four years. It runs alongside the Ark – a separate initiative specialising in treating younger children, run by charity NCH Action For Children. So far this year, Oxyap has had 20 referrals and there is now a waiting list for assessments that can run to several weeks. The project has just been awarded £10,000 government funding which will be used to increase staff and reduce waiting times.

Charities such as ChildLine, which every year receives thousands of calls from victims of child abuse, want to see more local authorities offering these specialist services. 'Research shows you can identify children who are abusing sexually and may go on to become an adult abuser, so positive work like this is very helpful,' says Hereward Harrison, ChildLine's director of policy. 'The younger they are identified the better. This can stop the horror and the devastation that comes from a career of abuse which ultimately ends with the abuser in prison.'

For Andrew Durham, the message is simple. 'If you can work with a person and change their development, you could be preventing quite a large number of future victims,' he says. 'Our work has only just begun. There will continue to be thousands more victims until every social services department includes these preventative measures in their child protection policies.'

• Sibs is on 01926-813110; Oxyap is on 01865-221201.

Child sexual abuse

Information from Barnardo's

The sexual abuse of children is not a rare occurrence. It happens at all social levels, in all parts of the country and in all races and cultures.

Despite increasing public awareness, the true extent of child sexual abuse remains hidden. Conservative estimates suggest that one child in ten will experience sexual abuse.

Key points

• Both girls and boys may be sexually abused
• Children of all ages may experience sexual abuse – from babies to teenagers
• Girls are more likely to be abused within the family, while boys are more likely to be abused outside it
• Children with disabilities are particularly vulnerable to sexual abuse
• Sexual abuse can occur as a single incident, but often involves a series of abusive acts
• Sexual abuse is rarely opportunistic: the abuse will usually have been planned over a period of time
• Child sexual abuse is an abuse of power by the person who abuses. Responsibility always lies with the abuser

• It is impossible to 'spot' an abuser: people who sexually abuse others come from all walks of life and usually appear no different from anyone else
• Abusers are most likely to be male and known to the victim
• There is growing evidence that females also sexually abuse children
• Children and young people may themselves be sexual abusers
• Children do not normally lie about being sexually abused, and should always be taken seriously
• Greater awareness and vigilance among adults and better social, health and sex education for young people is needed to protect children from abuse
• Too few cases of child sexual abuse, particularly of very young children, result in prosecution
• More support is needed for children who have been sexually abused to help prevent long-term emotional and psychological problems, and difficulties in forming relationships later in life.

• The above information is from a Barnardo's briefing. See page 41 for their address details.   © Barnardo's

How the police fail 'at risk' youngsters

By Stephen Wright

The lamentable state of child protection for 5,000 vulnerable youngsters in London was exposed in an explosive police report yesterday.

As the fall-out continues over the tragic death of Anna Climbie, the *Daily Mail* can reveal children are being placed at increased risk because poorly trained officers work under unsuitable conditions.

The secret study tells how under-funding throughout the capital means officers assigned to 'at risk' cases do not even have access to vital computer equipment. London's 23 child protection teams are said to be greatly under-staffed and, astonishingly, have access to just four pooled cars between them.

One team has been forced to work in an old mental hospital – where communications are described as 'primitive'. Details of the report, written by a senior Scotland Yard detective, will deepen the controversy surrounding the case of eight-year-old Anna, who died after being tortured by her great aunt and her boyfriend.

Eight police officers – including two inspectors – are under investigation for their handling of the case.

They include PC Karen Jones, the investigating officer, who friends claim has been made a scapegoat for mistakes made by social workers, hospital consultants and police. Detective Chief Superintendent Derek Kelleher, who heads the child protection operational command unit at Scotland Yard, wrote his dossier in September in the run-up to the court case. In it he says: 'Local authorities are aware and concerned about falling resources in child protection teams.'

Many teams do not have a single trained detective, he adds, referring directly to the Climbie case and the Haringey police child protection team.

'The incident has revealed no investigative experience was present within the team. No training is provided to CPT officers other than memorandum training (special procedures for interviewing juveniles).'

Mr Kelleher said child protection teams have become the 'Cinderellas' of the Met.

Children are being placed at increased risk because poorly trained officers work under unsuitable conditions

'They have been under-resourced. Nearly 50 per cent are not able to access Otis (the Met's computer system for reporting crime and reading intelligence files). At some sites that are equipped with Otis the local borough will not allow the CPT to plug in.

'The worst case is the Ealing Team housed inside St Bernard's mental hospital. The health authority was told it was a temporary situation. That was 12 years ago.

'The site is unsuitable. Communications support is primitive. IT is generally hand-me-downs.'

Since Anna Climbie's great aunt and boyfriend were convicted last Friday, attention has focused on the incompetence of agencies which could have prevented her death.

Blunders by three health authorities, two hospitals and up to eight police officers allowed Marie Therese Kouao, 44, and Carl Manning, 28, to subject Anna to the most cruel abuse imaginable.

She had come to Britain from the Ivory Coast for a better life. But within a year she died of neglect and hypothermia – under the noses of professionals who had been repeatedly alerted to her plight.

After her death, doctors found 128 separate injuries on her body.

So far, of those involved, only a social worker, Lisa Arthurworrey from Haringey Council, has been suspended from duty.

Eight police officers and a hospital consultant, Ruby Schwartz, criticised for their roles, have been allowed to stay in work while the Government inquiry is carried out.

Sexually abused?

Information from Young Minds

What is sexual abuse?

Sexual abuse can include different kinds of activities such as:

- Some types of kissing
- Touching private parts of the body
- Rape (being forced to have sex when you don't want to)
- Being made to look at porno-graphic videos or magazines
- Other acts which are felt by the child or young person to be abusive.

This is not the kind of sex play which is a normal part of growing up, when children and young people want to find out about each other's bodies, or when people start going out with each other.

Sexual abusers are usually stronger or in a position of power or authority over the child or young person. They use this power to get the person to take part in sexual activities.

The law tries to protect the safety and rights of children and young people. When someone sexually abuses a child or young person they are breaking the law.

Who sexually abuses children?

Abusers are not usually strangers. Most often, they are a relative, friend of the family, neighbour, a lodger, baby-sitter, someone at school, or even a group. Sometimes they can be other young people – a brother or sister or one of their friends. They often secretly abuse more than one child. Sexual abuse is usually carried out by men but sometimes women do it too.

How someone who has been abused might feel

Being abused leads to feelings which are hard to cope with, such as feeling: dirty; ashamed; depressed; worthless; frightened; worried about abusing others; confused; isolated; suicidal; angry; embarrassed; worried about sexuality; anxious; like running away;

scared about having a boyfriend or girlfriend; guilty; lonely.

'When I told him not to do it he said "Don't be silly, it's just a game, what do you mean you don't like it?" I felt really mixed up. Sometimes he would say "I'm doing this because I love you . . . it's our special secret OK?". I thought maybe it was just me. Maybe I just had the wrong feelings. Maybe all dads are like that and it's just me who's weird.'

The person carrying out the abuse may be someone who seems to be very nice in lots of ways. This can make it very hard to accept that they are capable of sexual abuse.

'I know this sounds really stupid now. But I thought that someone who abused people was horrible ALL the

time. I didn't think they were nice too, like helping you with your homework or buying you new clothes, normal stuff, so it took a while for the penny to drop.'

Some abusers choose to believe that there is nothing wrong in what they are doing. They may claim that those they abuse encourage them. This can cause people who are being abused a lot of confusing feelings, such as that they are to blame if they didn't tell the abuser not to do it, or if they didn't tell anyone. Many abusers rely on the age, inexperience and fear of people they abuse to be able to carry on with it.

'It all started after Dad died. I bottled up my feelings inside because Mum was really gutted. She had to work more shifts to earn enough money. Her brother looked after us in the evenings. That's when it started. He said if I told Mum, she would probably crack up because she's been through so much already.'

Child protection statistics

Children and young people on child protection registers in England at 31 March by category of abuse.

Category of abuse	1996	1997	1998	1999	2000
Neglect alone	8,724	9,511	10,300	11,100	11,100
Physical injury alone	8,703	8,154	7,300	6,500	5,900
Sexual abuse alone	5,935	5,575	4,900	4,800	3,800
Emotional abuse alone	4,973	5,072	5,200	5,400	5,500
Neglect, physical and sexual abuse	305	231	200	200	300
Neglect and physical injury	1,507	1,611	1,700	1,700	1,800
Neglect and sexual abuse	626	757	800	800	800
Physical injury and sexual abuse	862	776	700	700	700
Categories not recommended by 'Working Together'	527	414	300	500	300
No category available – transfer pending conferencing	189	178	200	200	100
Total of all abuse categories	32,351	32,369	31,600	31,900	30,300

Source: Department of Health. Children and young people on child protection registers, year ending 31 March 2000: England. London. Crown Copyright

Adults are responsible for looking after and protecting children and young people. Children are not responsible for protecting adults.

How abuse can affect behaviour

Sexual abuse can also lead to other problems: not taking care of yourself; bed-wetting; difficulty sleeping; bad dreams; running away; blanking out the memory; not being able to make friends; losing your temper; eating problems; self-harming; poor concentration; using alcohol or drugs.

'Before I told anyone, I was scared to go to sleep at night. Even though I tried not to think about what happened, I still had nightmares. I was too tired to bother with school and just wandered around on my own. I felt like an alien, the only one in the world like this, and I couldn't tell anyone.

Everything built up inside. I got into trouble for not doing my work, and ended up chucking a chair at someone. I was told I would be excluded if it happened again. Mum couldn't have coped with that. So I started cutting myself instead.'

People often do their best to cope with painful feelings by trying to forget about them. But this doesn't always work.

'I didn't know what to do, because I knew I'd always have to go home and face it. I thought if I could try not to think about it, squash it out of my mind it could be like it wasn't really happening. But stupid little things would remind me, make me feel horrible inside. My friends drifted away, and I started going round with people who were in trouble. We would walk out of school after registration, go shop-lifting, get drunk and play chicken. Why did I do it? Because for that moment, when I was taking a risk, I knew I wouldn't be thinking about home.'

Some people feel that the only way to manage what is happening is to run away from home. If this happens, they are in a lot of danger from people who will take advantage of them. It is easy to become involved in crime or prostitution. If you are feeling like this it is VERY IMPORTANT that you get help.

Sources of help

Some of these helplines can get very busy, but keep trying:

ChildLine
Freepost 1111
London N1 OBR
Tel: 0800 1111
www.childline.org.uk
24-hour helpline for children and young people providing confidential counselling, support and advice on any issue. You can also write to ChildLine. They will always write back.

NSPCC
National Centre
42 Curtain Road
London
Tel: 0800 800 500
Textphone: 0800 056 0566
www.nspcc.org.uk
Offers counselling, information and advice for anyone worried about a child at risk of abuse.

Children's Legal Centre
University of Essex
Wivenhoe Park, Colchester
CO4 3SQ
CLC@essex.ac.uk
Tel: 01206 873820
Monday 10am – 12pm
Monday – Friday 2 – 5pm
www2.essex.ac.uk/clc
Provides free legal advice and information for children and young people on any issue.

Youth Access
1a Taylors Yard
71 Alderbrook Road
London SW12 8AD
Tel: 020 8772 9900
Youth Access can give details of local advice, information and counselling services.

Sexwise
Network Scotland
The Mews, 57 Ruthven Lane
Glasgow G12 9JQ
Tel: 0800 28 29 30
Monday – Sunday 7am – Midnight
Provides information, advice and guidance for young people on various issues concerning peer pressure, relationships, contraception, pregnancy etc.

Get Connected
PO Box 21082, London
N1 9WW
Tel: 0800 096 0096
Monday – Friday 4pm – 11.30pm
For young people who are thinking of running away, or who have run away. Helps young people work out what they need most when they phone, and puts them in touch with places that can help.

Samaritans
Tel: 08457 90 90 90
Open 24 hours a day
jo@samaritans.org.uk
or if you want to remain anonymous:
samaritans@anon.twwells.co
www.samaritans.org.uk
Offers emotional support to anyone going through any problem.

Careline
Tel: 020 8514 1177
Monday – Friday
10am – 4pm, 7pm – 10pm
Confidential counselling for anyone on any issue.

London Rape Crisis Centre
PO Box 69, London WC1X 9JN
Tel: 020 7837 1600
Monday – Friday 6pm – 10pm
Saturday – Sunday 10am – 10pm
Offers advice, information, counselling to women and girls anywhere in the UK who have been raped or sexually abused, their friends, families, partners and professionals.

- The above information is an excerpt from the YoungMinds booklet *Sexually Abused?* details of which can be found on their web site at www.youngminds.org.uk Alternatively, see page 41 for their address details.

© *YoungMinds*

Kidscape keepsafe code

Information from Kidscape

1. Hugs

Hugs and kisses are nice, especially from people we like. Even hugs and kisses that feel good and that you like should never be kept secret.

2. Body

Your body belongs to you and not to anyone else. This means all of your body, particularly the private parts covered by your swim suit. If anyone ever tries to touch your body in a way which confuses or frightens you, say NO and tell.

3. No

If anyone older than you, even someone you know, tries to kiss or touch you in a way you don't like or that confuses you, or which they say is supposed to be a secret, say NO in a very loud voice. Don't talk to anyone you don't know when you are alone, or just with other children. You don't have to be rude, just pretend you didn't hear and keep on walking.

4. Run

If a stranger, or a bully, or even someone you know tries to harm you or touch you in a frightening way, run away and get help. Make sure you always run towards other people or to a shop, if you can.

5. Yell

Wherever you are, it is all right to yell if someone is trying to hurt you. Practise yelling as loud as you can in a big, deep voice by taking a deep breath and letting the yell come from your stomach, not from your throat.

6. Tell

Tell a grown-up you trust if anyone frightens you or tries to touch you in a way which makes you feel unsafe. It is never your fault, if an older person does this.

If the first grown-up you tell doesn't believe you, keep telling until someone does. It might not be easy, but even if something has already happened that you have never told before, try to tell now. Who could you tell?

7. Secrets

Secrets such as surprise birthday parties are fun. But some secrets are not good and should never be kept. No older person should ever ask you to keep a kiss, hug or touch secret. If anyone does, even if you know that person, tell a grown-up you trust.

8. Bribes

Don't accept money or sweets or a gift from anyone without first checking with your parents. Most of the time it will be all right, like when you get a present for your birthday from your grandma. But some people try to trick children into doing something by giving them sweets or money. This is called a bribe… don't ever take one!

Remember, it is possible that you might have to do what a bully or older person tells you, so that you can keep yourself safe. Don't feel bad if that happens because the most important thing is for you to be safe.

9. Code

Have a code word or sign with your parents or guardians, which only you and they know. If they need to send someone to collect you, they can give that person the code. Don't tell the code to anyone else.

10. D.I.Y.

What are your own ideas to keep safe?

Kidscape extra

- Don't answer the door if you are at home on your own.
- Don't tell anyone over the telephone that you are at home alone. Say that your mum will ring back, she's in the bath – or any other excuse you can think of.
- Always tell your parents or whoever is taking care of you where you are going and how you can be contacted.
- If you get lost, go to a shop or a place with lots of people, and ask for help or find a policeman or policewoman to ask.
- Travel in a carriage of a train where there are other people.
- When you're out on your own, keep far enough away from people you don't know so that you can't be grabbed and so can run away.
- Never play in deserted or dark places.
- Carry enough money for your return trip home and never spend it on anything else.
- Memorise your telephone number and address.
- Know how to contact your parents or a neighbour.
- If you have no money, but need to ring home in an emergency, dial 100 and ask the operator to place a reverse charge call.
- To make an emergency telephone call:
  1. Dial 999 (you don't need to put money in a coin box phone), the operator will say, 'which service?'
  2. You say 'police, fire or ambulance'.
  3. They put you through to the service, who will take your name and where you are, so they can find you. Then you tell them what's wrong. This sounds like it would take a long time, but it happens very quickly. The operator listens in case of difficulty.
- Always get an adult to make an emergency telephone call, if possible. NO ONE should ever make one unless there is a real emergency.

• The above information is an extract from Kidscape's publication *Keep them Safe*. See page 41 for their address details.

© Reproduced with kind permission from Kidscape

Don't talk to anyone you don't know when you are alone, or just with other children

---

Dealing with suspected abuse

Information from the NSPCC

It is one of the most difficult things for a parent to deal with when they discover that their child has been abused. It strikes at the heart of the parent's wish to protect their child and can raise all kinds of painful feelings such as 'How didn't I know what was happening to my child?', 'Didn't my child trust me enough to tell me?'

Children often communicate their worries or distress through their behaviour, and it is sometimes through changes in their child's behaviour that parents become aware that something might be wrong. It is important to remember that there are many things that might be worrying a child such as whether they are having difficulties in school or whether there have been any changes in the family. However, if they have been abused, there might be all sorts of reasons why a child might be frightened to speak about what has happened to them, so it is important to talk to them, giving lots of reassurance that whatever they might say, their parents will always love them.

Taking in what has been said can be devastating, and raises all sorts of feelings for the parents. However difficult this is, it is important to allow the child to tell their story. The way that a child deals with their abuse depends on many factors. However, a key one is the response he or she gets when they tell what has happened to them. If they feel believed, understood and reassured, then they will be much more able to deal with what has happened. If they feel doubted or blamed for what has happened, this can compound the effects of the abuse.

If a child has been abused, then the next step is to report this to the appropriate authorities, which are the local social services department or the police. These agencies work together to support and help families in these circumstances and also to consider whether there is a case for

NSPCC ⬤
Cruelty to children must stop. FULL STOP.

prosecuting the abuser. Often this step is worrying for parents. Sometimes the concerns relate to the abuser being a family member and many people fear possible rifts in the family. These are complex and difficult issues, and often people want to talk these issues through. There are also potentially longer-term issues that might arise. For instance, the child might need some kind of therapeutic help to help them deal with what has happened.

If a child has been abused, then the next step is to report this to the appropriate authorities

---

It can be helpful to contact the NSPCC Child Protection Helpline to discuss all these issues. If you would like to speak to somebody about this, then ring the Helpline on 0808 800 5000. As well as discussing the situation and offering advice, Child Protection Telephone Counsellors can refer any concerns about abuse to the local Social Services Department or police. There is also a textphone for people who are hard of hearing or deaf. The number for this is 0800 056 0566. It is also possible to email the Helpline on help@nspcc.org.uk.

You could also contact the following organisations as other possible sources of help:

MOSAC
141 Greenwich High Road, London, SE10 8JA. Tel: 0800 980 1958. Telephone advice, information and support for mothers and female carers of children who have been sexually abused. Offer a sympathetic ear, befriending and practical support.

Family Matters
13 Wrotham Road, Gravesend, Kent, DA11 0PA. Tel: 01474 537392. In addition to services for children (from 14 years old), adolescents and adults who have been victims of abuse, this agency also offers services for non-abusing family members.

• The above information is from the NSPCC's web site which can be found at www.nspcc.org.uk

© NSPCC

Government to allow smacking by childminders

By Richard Garner,
Education Editor

The Government is to press ahead with a controversial move to allow childminders to smack children in their care.

Regulations will be laid before Parliament early next week permitting carers to smack children and smoke in front of them provided they have the consent of parents. The move, which provoked an outcry from childcare groups after being suggested in a consultation paper late last year, was condemned by Labour and Conservative MPs when revealed at a meeting of the Commons Select Committee on Education yesterday.

Margaret Hodge, minister for Education and Employment with responsibility for the under-fives, rejected opposition by childcare groups, saying: 'Most if not all parents care deeply about their kids and the judgement that some other professional can make a better judgement about a behaviour code is wrong.'

Ms Hodge said a poll of parents by the Government had revealed that 83 per cent wanted to be free to draw up a code of conduct with their childminder. 'If this is what they feel, then what right has the Government got to say we as politicians know better?' she added.

Nick St Aubyn, Conservative member for Guildford, argued: 'Isn't the problem that parents don't know enough about the consequences that may occur if they don't take the right attitude on this issue?

'If it is felt necessary that childminders put a seat belt on any child in the back of a car, then surely it is wrong to allow them to smack children and smoke in front of them?'

Barry Sheerman, Labour chairman of the committee, said: 'There was a unanimous view of this committee that you are wrong on this issue. I would hate to use your logic when it comes to capital punishment. There is a clear majority there for it in polls but we as politicians have said that's not the way we want to go.'

> **'If this is what they feel, then what right has the Government got to say we as politicians know better?'**

But Ms Hodge replied: 'There is a realm of difference between deliberately taking an act which takes someone's life and whether or not you have a code which allows a childminder to smoke in front of a child or smack them. We all know there is a vast difference between child abuse and smacking.'

Ms Hodge told MPs that a growing number of men were applying for jobs in child care or nursery schools. Figures showed that 8 per cent of those who responded to a government campaign for recruits were men.

The minister added: 'I think we are raising the status of child care and that may be why we are getting more men showing an interest.' She told MPs that the Government 'hasn't yet caught up with our European partners' over the provision of child care despite doubling the budget from £1bn to £2bn since taking office. The Government was planning to create 200,000 new nursery places by 2004.

Internet ban puts children in their place

By Nicole Martin

Banning naughty children from using the internet has replaced a smack or locking them in their room without any supper, a report says today.

This 'virtual punishment' is also fast replacing extra chores and the withholding of pocket money, says the report published by the Family Assurance Group, a family society based in Brighton.

However, the most effective punishment is grounding: a curfew on all social activities for up to a week. This is closely followed by withdrawing all treats, including watching television.

John Reeve, the chief executive of the Family Assurance Group, said the study, in which 10,000 parents were questioned, showed that adults had been forced to abandon the old-fashioned tactics that had worked with them.

'Modern deterrents' were needed to punish 'modern childen', he said. 'Gone are the severest sanctions that the older generation still recall with trembling lips and quaking knees. Thankfully, for many of today's youngsters, the threat of the slipper has been overtaken by cessation of social pleasures. The ultimate sanction is to force children to stay at home.'

Childminders and smacking

Parents back informal agreements on smacking with childminders rather than government rules

Parents have given overwhelming backing to the Government's view that parents – rather than Whitehall – should decide with childminders whether or not they are allowed to smack children in their care or smoke in their presence within their own home.

Eighty-three per cent of parents think that parents should be the ones to decide whether their childminder should be permitted to smack their child. Only 10 per cent of parents think that the Government should decide. Seventy-four per cent of parents think that parents should be the ones to decide whether their childminder should be able to smoke in the presence of their child. Only 20 per cent of parents think that the Government should decide.

The backing came in an independent opinion poll by RSGB of a representative sample of 1,000 parents and has led Employment and Equal Opportunities Minister Margaret Hodge to confirm that parents will continue to be free to decide whether their childminders should be permitted to smack their children or to smoke in their presence within their own home.

The Government will ban smoking or smacking in daycare settings, such as nurseries, crèches and out-of-school clubs, or in settings which receive Nursery Education Grant. This ban in these settings will reinforce the Government's focus on good quality provision, backed by our strong record on child protection.

Mrs Hodge said: 'The Government has been consulting on new national standards for daycare – the first time any government has attempted to set national minimum standards in this area. We have carefully considered the views of parents, childminders and professional associations in the consultation.

'We need to strike the right

balance between the freedom of parents to determine how their childminders care for children in private homes and the views of some childcare groups who want childminders treated the same as other providers.

'Our instincts were that parents would support the balance which we had suggested, but we wanted to hear their views. It is clear that the overwhelming majority think that these matters should be decided through private, written agreements between the parent and childminder. Of course, every childminder is free to have a no smacking or no smoking policy.

'This is a powerful message from parents that they want to be free to make their own arrangements with childminders. This is putting the decision where it should be – with the parents.'

Notes

This press notice relates to England
1. Independent pollsters RSGB asked 1031 parents (including 797 in England) of 0-10-year-olds the following questions (only one answer was allowed for each question):

'Nowadays most types of childcare have to meet standards set by Government. For example, people working in day nurseries, nursery schools and playgroups are not allowed to smack children or smoke in their presence.

The Government is introducing new national standards for childcare. Today we want to ask you some questions about childminders in particular.

Registered childminders provide care in their own home and often discuss with parents how their children should be looked after.

The following questions are about what the Government should decide and what should be left to individual parents.

Q1. Who do you think should decide whether, in certain circumstances, childminders can smack children in their care?

The parent in agreement with the childminder 83% (in England); 84% (for UK)

The Government by setting national standards 10% (England); 10% (for UK)

No strong views either way 7% (England); 6% (for UK)

Q2. Who do you think should decide whether childminders can smoke in the presence of children in their care?

The parent in agreement with the childminder 74% (in England); 75% (for UK)

The Government by setting national standards 20% (in England); 19% (for UK)

No strong views either way 6% (in England); 6% (for UK)'

2. DfEE officials consulted with over 70 different groups and organisations during the formulation of the proposed standards, including

> **'This is a powerful message from parents that they want to be free to make their own arrangements with childminders'**

current regulators and individual day care providers. A number of national organisations working in the early years sector were also involved. Initial analysis of 335 responses to the consultation (specifically on the

standards relating to childminders) shows 39 per cent of respondents disagreed with the proposal to allow childminders to smoke; on smacking it was 48 per cent disagreeing.

3. The new standards will establish a consistent approach across the country, replacing the variations that apply currently in each of the 150 local authorities. They will set the context for regulation of the sector by OFSTED under Part VI of the Care Standards Act 2000 when responsibility transfers from local authorities in September 2001.

© Crown copyright 1995-2000

What's wrong with smacking?

Information from EPOCH

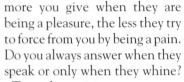

It's wrong for adults to hit adults and wrong for children to hit children or adults. So it must be wrong for adults to hit children.

Children learn right from wrong by copying parents. If you hit them they'll think it's OK to hit people smaller than themselves. If you don't want them to think it's ever right to hit, don't ever hit them. Even if they've hit or hurt somebody, two wrongs can't make a right.

Smacking does not help children learn how to behave

A smack shows you are angry but not what you are angry about.

Smacked children will not hear if you try to explain – how can they listen while they cry?

Even if they do hear they will not feel like trying to please you: smacks hurt and humiliate children so they are more likely to make them angry than sorry.

Good discipline means working with your children, not against them . . .

Remember you're the grown-up. Your children are your apprentices in learning how to behave: show and tell them how it's done.

- Keep them safe while they grow: give them secure limits they can test but not overturn. Make sure the baby can't reach the fire; the toddler cannot open that

forbidden gate; the older child is holding your hand before you reach the road.

- Keep them secure while they learn: give them their say, listen to them, respect their point of view, but don't let them bore or blackmail you into giving in against your better judgement.
- Children need your attention and will do anything to get it. The

more you give when they are being a pleasure, the less they try to force from you by being a pain. Do you always answer when they speak or only when they whine?

Try to be positive:

'Do' works better than 'don't': rewards work better than punishments.

- Show and tell what they *should* do – not just what they shouldn't.
- *Explain* your real reasons – 'because I say so' teaches nothing for next time.
- Try to say '*yes*' and 'well done' at least as often as '*no*' and 'stop that'.
- Be as ready to *praise* behaviour you like as to *scold* for behaviour you don't.
- Rely on *rewards* like hugs and jokes, not *punishments* like smacks and yells.
- *Ignore* minor silliness and 'cheek'. The more you nag the less they'll listen.
- When they do something wrong explain what it is and *how to put things right*.
- Even when you *dislike* your child's behaviour, *never suggest that you dislike your child*.

• The above information is from EPOCH. See page 41 for their address details.

© EPOCH

Why should physical punishment be banned?

Information from Children are Unbeatable!

Why do we need full legal reform to end all corporal punishment? In response to the 1998 judgment of the European Court of Human Rights concerning the repeated caning of a young boy by his stepfather (*A v UK*), the UK Government accepted that the law must be changed to give children better protection. In January 2000 the Government launched a consultation on how to change the law – but it only proposed new ways to define in law what kind of corporal punishment of children is acceptable. The next step is likely to be a Parliamentary Bill introducing law reform in this area; an amendment to outlaw corporal punishment would probably have a free 'conscience' vote.

The 'Children are Unbeatable!' Alliance calls for a ban on all forms of physical punishment. The Alliance numbers over 300 organisations (including the Royal Colleges representing paediatricians, psychiatrists and general practitioners, Women's Aid Federations, the NSPCC, churches and many parent-support agencies) as well as many prominent individuals. The Alliance recognises that parents who smack are usually acting with good intentions according to social expectations. The aim is not to denounce or prosecute parents, but simply to move society along – just as we have moved on from condoning the hitting of wives or servants.

The Alliance submitted a detailed response to the Government consultation, published on behalf of the Alliance by the NSPCC: *Moving on from smacking*.

The Government has cited public opinion, based on poll findings, as justification for its position (though in fact its own poll shows the public is much less tolerant of physical punishment than the Government). In fact, a 1999 MORI poll found that the Alliance's position commanded strong support (73% of the general public, even higher for parents) – if those polled could be sure that trivial smacks would not be prosecuted.

The Alliance believes that on this issue the Government needs to lead public opinion rather than follow it. Evidence from the 10 European countries that have banned smacking is that public opinion quickly catches up with legal reform.

A ban on all forms of corporal punishment is needed in order to:

Enhance child protection:
First, by easing prosecution in cases in which it is plainly necessary in the interests of the child; second, by enabling child protection workers to give parents of children at risk of abuse a clear message that no level of corporal punishment is acceptable; third, by ensuring that children have a consistent level of protection which does not vary according to where they are placed or who is caring for them, and fourth, by preventing unintended physical or psychological injury;

support parents:
by providing a clear legal basis for the promotion of positive, non-violent forms of discipline by statutory and voluntary bodies working with families – discipline which reduces stress, improves family relationships and creates sociable, self-disciplined and well-motivated children;

tackle violence and crime:
because corporal punishment is a significant factor in the development of violent behaviour in childhood and later life, clear reform would help measures to reduce violence and crime. It would also help to promote the concept of zero tolerance of violence between all family members and thus reduce all forms of domestic violence, and it would help reduce bullying between children;

assert the equal human right of children to protection of their physical integrity:
this is a protection which all adults take for granted. Challenging routine violence to children, the weakest members of society, is as important

to them as challenging routine violence to women has been to improving women's status. The UN Convention on the Rights of the Child requires the UK to protect children from 'all forms of physical or mental violence'. The international monitoring body for the Convention, the Committee on the Rights of the Child, has emphasised that physical punishment within the family is not compatible with full implementation, and has formally recommended prohibition to the UK and to many other countries.

Myths about the campaign to ban smacking

This is a debate which raises a number of anxieties and questions. Some false allegations have also been made about the effects of banning smacking, and in particular about what has happened in Sweden in the twenty years following the outlawing of smacking. A detailed review of the available Swedish data has been published on behalf of the Alliance by Save the Children UK. Some of these findings are given below, in which we seek to clear up misunderstandings.

Outlawing smacking:

would not lead to the prosecution of parents for trivial smacks – any more than adults are prosecuted for trivial assaults on other adults.

On the contrary, clear reform coupled with education is likely to reduce the need for prosecutions through changes in parental attitudes and practice. This has happened in Sweden, where there has been no increase in prosecutions for parental assaults of children since the ban (the strongest decline being shown in relation to parents in their twenties – who were themselves brought up without smacking).

would not lead to more compulsory social work intervention in families or removals of children into care.

Again the Swedish experience shows a marked decline in out-of-family placements of children and of compulsory forms of intervention. The grounds for social work assistance, care orders or supervision orders under the Children Act would be unaffected by legal reform.

would not prevent parents from using physical measures to protect or restrain their children, nor absolve them of their duty to teach children good manners, the difference between right and wrong, and how to behave thoughtfully and respectfully towards others.

Indeed, one can anticipate greater use of positive, consistent and effective forms of discipline as a consequence of such a ban. (A recent National Family and Parenting Institute poll found only one in five parents believing smacking was an effective way of teaching right from wrong.)

would not be a 'pointless' or 'unenforceable' measure.

Although there is no increase in official state intervention in families, there have been significant changes in attitudes and practice in countries which have adopted a ban. A majority supported smacking in Sweden before the ban, now only 6% of under-35-year-olds support even the mildest form of physical punishment. On the other hand, there is no evidence that physical punishment will disappear of its own accord. The prevalence of corporal punishment in the family, including 'severe' corporal punishment, remains very high in the UK. Recent Government-commissioned research involved interviews with over 400 families. It found that 97% of the four-year-olds were physically punished, almost half more than once a week. Three-quarters of the one-year-old babies were smacked in their first year. Almost a quarter of seven-year-olds had experienced 'severe' punishment by mothers (defined as involving 'intention or potential to cause injury or psychological damage, use of implements, repeated actions or over a long period of time').

The Government consultation on changing the law on physical punishment

(The consultations for England and Wales were issued on 16 January 2000 with a three-month consultation period, closing 21 April 2000; the Scottish Executive consultation was issued in February 2000, closing on 21 April 2000. The full text is available on their respective websites.)

The Department of Health consultation document, *Protecting Children, Supporting Parents*, asked only four questions which were hard to answer from the Alliance standpoint as the questions presupposed that some level of physical punishment was acceptable. Alliance members were advised to make clear that their replies did not mean that they condoned the Government's minimalist approach.

The 'minimum' reform

The document starts with the Government's proposals for 'the minimum steps needed' for reform, which were not open to consultation. These are as follows:

first, to set out the legal defence of 'reasonable chastisement' in written law and second, to require courts to have regard to a short checklist of factors ('nature and context of the treatment; its duration; its physical and mental effects; and, in some instances, the sex, age and state of health of the victim') when deciding whether punishment is 'reasonable'.

Comment: The Government is not consulting on this basic reform – why not? In the European Human Rights Court case the UK court did consider all the above factors, so this reform would have made no difference to that case and thus cannot be the minimum necessary to remedy it. Also, the Government should surely seek to prevent such chastisement occurring, not just to secure findings of guilt in prosecutions. The law needs to give clear messages to parents. A checklist of abstract factors is useless to parents.

Respondents were then asked to answer four questions on possible additional reforms:

Question 1. What, if any, factors over and above these factors should courts consider?
Comment: As stated above, this approach does nothing to improve things. One factor that must be excluded is what the child did to merit punishment, as the European Court has held this to be irrelevant.

Question 2. Should the law state that the following forms of physical punishment are never reasonable: punishment which causes, or is likely to cause, injuries to the head (including brain, eyes and ears); punishment using implements (e.g. canes, slippers, belts)?
Comment: It is shocking to be asked if causing a brain or eye injury could ever be reasonable! Of course these should be banned, but why stop there? What about shaking? What about injuries to mouth, nose, teeth, genitals and all other erogenous zones, fingers, toes, central nervous system, heart, lungs, stomach, kidneys and so on? What about psychological injury? What about blows with a closed fist? What about biting, kicking or pinching? What about infants? (We note the poll, commissioned by the Department of Health and quoted in the consultation document, found overwhelming support for banning smacking of under-twos.)

Question 3. Should the defence of reasonable chastisement be unavailable to those charged with 'actual bodily harm' (defined as 'loss or breaking of a tooth, temporary loss of sensory functions including loss of consciousness; extensive or multiple bruising; displaced broken nose; minor fractures; minor cuts requiring medical treatment (e.g. stitches); and psychiatric injury which is more than fear, distress or panic') and more serious assaults?
Comment: One should hope that injuries of this severity are always successfully prosecuted at present. Certainly the boy in the European court case did not suffer this degree of harm and it is therefore plain the European judgment requires the Government to ban punishment which is much less severe than 'actual bodily harm' (ABH). Less than four per cent of the Department of Health poll found punishment reasonable if it causes a red mark that lasts for a few days, and less than 1 per cent condoned

a bruise that lasts a few days. This proposal also might well create a dangerous presumption that any injury below the level of ABH is reasonable.

Question 4. Who should be allowed to physically punish children? Everyone who looks after them unless specifically prohibited by law (as now)? Parents only? Parents, plus those with express permission from parents?
Comment: This is a reminder that the law on physical punishment in non-family placements is still unsatisfactory. For example, smacking is prohibited in nurseries, but not for childminding or crèches, nor in private fostering. Research shows that children are often abused by adults in their household who are not their parents. Obviously the limited response to this unsatisfactory question has to be parents only.

• The above information is from Children are Unbeatable!'s web site which can be found at www.childrenareunbeatable.org.uk
© Children are Unbeatable!

Hitting people is wrong

And children are people too

It is time to end physical punishment of children worldwide because:
- Hitting children is a violation of their fundamental rights as people and a constant confirmation of their low status.
- It is a dangerous practice, sometimes causing serious 'accidental' injuries or escalating into behaviour recognised as child abuse.
- It encourages violent attitudes and behaviour both in childhood and later life – violence breeds violence.
- And it teaches the world's children nothing positive.

What is physical punishment?
Any punishment in which physical force is intended to cause pain or discomfort: hitting children with a hand, or with a cane, strap or other object, kicking, shaking or throwing children, scratching, pinching or pulling their hair, locking or tying them up.

English and some other languages have special words like 'smacking' and 'spanking' which tend to suggest that physical punishment of children is different from other forms of violence. Phrases like 'a good smack', 'six of the best' reflect societies' unique approval of it.

There are other harmful and humiliating kinds of punishment, of course, but physical punishment is our focus because it is clearly defined, frequently used, its harmful effects have been well demonstrated, and in most societies children are the only people who are not protected from it. Changing attitudes to physical punishment, and hence to children, will discourage other harmful forms of punishment.

Challenging parents', other carers' and teachers' rights to hit children often provokes emotional reactions. That is not surprising. Where physical punishment is common, it is a habit passed down from one generation to another, part of the child-rearing culture, and often of religious belief. People's own experiences as children, and as parents, get in the way of compassionate and logical consideration of the arguments.

But the UN Convention and other human rights charters with worldwide application make it clear that the world considers the right to physical integrity to be an absolute right, one which neither culture nor religion, tradition nor material circumstances should limit.

Those who campaign to end physical punishment of children are not just promoting one way of child-rearing over another: they are seeking to apply a fundamental human right to all adult/child relationships.

• The above information is from EPOCH. See page 41 for their address details.
©EPOCH

Protect children from paedophiles!

Advice and information for parents

Protect children!

Parents who contact Kidscape are worried about the best way to protect children, especially when they are out on their own. This article gives practical advice for keeping children safe and information on how paedophiles (people who sexually abuse children) target children.

Who are paedophiles?

- Paedophiles may seem perfectly respectable and 'nice'. They are extremely cunning and clever at worming their way into your confidence so that you trust them alone with your children.
- Paedophiles do not necessarily look dirty, weird or creepy or act suspiciously – they often behave like everyone else and look 'normal'.
- Paedophiles come from all classes, professions, racial and religious backgrounds.
- The majority of known paedophiles are male, though some women abuse children.
- 66% of paedophiles are known to the child, 34% are strangers.

What paedophiles say

This information comes from the paedophiles themselves, who told Kidscape how they ensnare children.

- Paedophiles are good at making friends with children. They offer to teach them games, sports or how to play a musical instrument. They take them on outings, give them gifts, bribes, toys, money or treats and trick children into trusting them.
- Paedophiles often target single-parent families where mothers might be especially grateful for help with looking after the children.

- 48% of the paedophiles found their victims through baby-sitting.
- 30% of the paedophiles had *each* committed offences against 10 to 450 victims, 70% had between 1 to 10 victims.
- Paedophiles find victims by hanging round places children are likely to go, such as:
  – arcades
  – school premises
  – shopping centres
  – amusement or theme parks
  – playgrounds
  – parks
  – swimming baths
  – fairs
  – fast food chains
- Be suspicious if someone is more interested in your children than in you, someone who always wants to baby-sit, take your children on outings – someone who wants to get your children alone.

What parents can do

- Check on anyone who is left in charge of your children or wants to spend time alone with them, especially baby-sitters. Talk (not just write) to other people they have worked for.
- Encourage discussions about personal safety, getting lost, and bullying by playing 'What if?' games with children.
- Practise the Kidscape rule 'Yell, Run, Tell' with children so they feel confident about using safety strategies.
- Explain to children the difference between 'safe' and 'unsafe' secrets. A secret about a surprise birthday party is OK, but *no one* should ever ask them to keep kisses or touches secret.
- Buy your children a Travelcard and/or Phonecard so that they can always call you or get home.
- Arrange to have a family code-word. Tell your child that if

anyone ever tries to collect them for you, the person will always know the codeword. 'No Code, No Go.'

- When visiting public places (shopping centres, funfairs) always arrange a meeting place with your child in case you get separated ('I will meet you outside Marks & Spencer' or 'by the fountain').
- Most paedophiles are not strangers. Tell children that if anyone, even *someone they know*, touches them in a confusing or frightening way they should tell you.

Tell your children

- To be wary of public toilets and to go in with a friend, if possible. If anyone approaches you, get out fast. (Parents – don't be embarrassed to stand outside the toilet and shout in 'Are you all right in there?' puts paedophiles right off!)
- If someone you don't know speaks to you, pretend you haven't heard and walk quickly away.
- Never take sweets, presents, or lifts from people you don't know.
- Never go up to a car to give directions – keep away so that no one can get hold of you and you can run away.
- If something bad does happen to you, even if you have broken a rule, you should tell me about it and I will help sort things out. (One child was walking in a park when told not to and was molested – she was afraid to tell because she had broken the rule about being in the park.)

Children should make a fuss!

- If someone tries to touch or grab you, shout 'NO', get away as fast as you can and then tell an adult.
- Practise the Kidscape rule: 'Yell, Run, Tell'.
- Remember, if someone frightens you, it is okay to break rules, shout or make a fuss.
- Always run towards shops or places with people.
- If you think that you are being followed, go into a shop or knock on the door of a house – ask for help.
- Break any rule to keep safe. Even

break a window to attract attention, if necessary.

Play safe

- Never play in dark or lonely places, or in empty streets and stairwells.
- Stay with friends or with a group and don't wander off on your own, even if you're playing hide and seek – hide with a friend.
- If you are in a shopping centre, arcade or disco and someone offers you money to do a job or errand, don't do it – it could be a trick.
- Don't walk to and from school on your own – team up with a friend or a group.
- Always tell your parents where you're going and when you'll be back.

Getting lost

- Learn your own address, telephone number and postcode.
- If you get lost, go into a shop or a place with lots of people and ask for help, or find a police officer, a security guard, or a traffic warden to ask. If you can't find a shop assistant or a person in a uniform, ask a man or a woman with children to help you.
- Don't go into a house, or office, or phonebox with anyone – wait outside while they telephone your parents or the police.
- Don't get into a car or accept a lift from anyone – say you'll wait for your parents or the police to fetch you.

Travelling alone

- Travel in a train carriage with other people.
- Carry enough money for your return trip and *never* spend it on anything else.
- Work out what you would do if you missed your train or a bus. How would you get home? Is there someone you could call?

Telephones

- Know how to use a public call box and how to contact your parents or whoever takes care of you.
- Know how to make an emergency phone call.
- You don't need money to make a reverse charge call (the person at the other end pays the bill).
- Carry a Phonecard so that you can always call home if you get stuck somewhere.

What if something happens?

- Be aware of changes in your child's behaviour which might indicate that something is not right (See Kidscape *Child Abuse: Signs and Symptoms* leaflet).
- If your child doesn't want to be with someone, find out why. Children may say things like, 'I don't want you to go out tonight', when they really mean 'I don't want to be left with the baby-sitter'.
- Stay calm and try not to transmit anger, shock or embarrassment to your child.
- Ensure that your child knows you believe him/her.
- Tell children it is NEVER their fault if someone abuses them.
- Praise your child for having told you and for 'getting through the ordeal'. Tell them you love them.
- Seek help for the child and yourself.

Free Kidscape safety guides

Child Abuse: Signs and Symptoms
Good Sense Defence for the Young
Keep Them Safe
Why My Child? – Advice for parents of children who have been sexually abused

For a free copy of these safety guides or for our free anti-bullying guides and details of our books and schools safety programmes, send a large, stamped, addressed envelope to: Kidscape, 2 Grosvenor Gardens, London SW1W 0DH. Tel: 0207 730 3300.

Kidscape is the only national charity teaching children about keeping safe before they become victims of abuse or bullying. Kidscape's message is prevention.

© Reproduced with kind permission from Kidscape

Eyes wide open

In the US, anyone can access the names and addresses of sex offenders, but while child murders there continue to rise, in the UK the figures remain low. Kendra Inman reports

Parents in Benton County in South Carolina know what predatory sex offenders look like. At any time of the day or night they can visit the community notification page on the Benton Sheriff's website and check through the gallery of convicted sex offenders living in their area.

They range from 28-year-old Kenneth Ray Davis, who targets young boys, to 71-year-old Jerry Lee Ray who abuses girls. Both offenders are on parole and banned from having contact with minors including visiting playgrounds, arcades and other places frequented by children.

This is the American way of protecting children. In the UK pressure is mounting for a 'Sarah's law', named after the murdered eight-year-old Sarah Payne, to establish a sex offenders' register open to the public. The move would be a British version of the US Megan's Law that allows communities access to the names and addresses of sex offenders.

As ministers decide whether more legislation is necessary, a British academic claims the US measures fail to protect children, and that ministers should give greater protection to children in the UK by ploughing more money into anti-poverty initiatives.

Professor Colin Pritchard, of Southampton University, points to World Health Organisation figures published last month on child homicides in the western world. In the US, where the number of adult murders has fallen, the number of children being killed has continued to rise, up 58% over the past five years, even after the introduction of Megan's Law, while in England and Wales we have seen the biggest reduction in child homicide in the western world, he says. Pritchard believes that our child protection system, although far from perfect, is succeeding in protecting children.

By Kendra Inman

'In 1974 at the time of the inquiry into the death of Maria Colwell, when the UK was waking up to child abuse, this country was the third highest child killer in the western world. Now we're the fifth lowest,' he says.

In the UK pressure is mounting for a 'Sarah's law', named after the murdered eight-year-old Sarah Payne, to establish a sex offenders' register open to the public

As the welfare state has been rolled back, so the child murder rate in the US has risen, says Pritchard. 'Under Reagan and Bush, they began to dismantle the welfare services. Although we had cuts, we did preserve our child protection services,' he says.

It is often said that 'stranger danger' is not the biggest threat to children – most die at the hand of someone they are close to. Pritchard says most child murderers are in a parental role. 'In the UK in the two years 1996-97, 110 children were killed. Just 19 were killed by a stranger. And for every child homicide, four children are killed in traffic accidents on the roads.'

He explains: 'We know that most child sex abuse of a damaging kind takes place in families, often poor families. We also know that the nasty malevolent stranger exists. But he targets disadvantaged children – those in poverty are more vulnerable to the lure of the stranger offering them gifts and treats.'

By tackling child poverty, we would be cutting the number of children vulnerable to abuse, inside and outside the home, he argues. He points to Sure Start, the government's programme to improve the chances of pre-school babies and children as one answer. 'But Sure Start will only be applied to a third of the country,' he says. 'It needs to be available to all struggling families.'

Fellow academic Professor Nigel Parton, from the University of Huddersfield, has written widely on child protection. He agrees that investing in Sure Start would do more to protect children than a 'Sarah's law'.

However, he stops short of drawing a direct correlation between poverty and abuse. 'You can't lump all child abuse in together. For example, there are issues around sexual abuse that are unique to that form of abuse – not just its emotional impact, but in the circumstances that surround it,' he says.

Not everyone supports Pritchard's theory that the success of child protection systems can be judged by murder rates. In the past his approach has attracted criticism from the NSPCC, among others.

In a recent statement, the charity said that communities have a right to know if paedophiles living in their area pose a serious risk to their children. Although it recognises that 'unmanaged forms of community notification can result in dangerous vigilante actions, mistaken identity and harm inflicted

Dispelling some myths

In 1998-99 in the UK, there were a total of 26 murders of children aged 5-16 years old, 24 of toddlers aged between one and under five years old and 45 babies under one year. Of these, around six or seven children per year are killed by a stranger and the numbers are not increasing, according to Home Office figures.

In the UK, fewer young children than ever before, aged 0-4, are being killed by abusers, says Professor Colin Pritchard. World Health Organisation statistics show that in the four years from 1974-78, 38 young children per million population died. By 1993-97 this had fallen to 15 – a drop of 61%. Similar falls were also seen in Japan, which saw a drop of 61%, and Germany, down 54%. In the US, 38 young children per million population died between 1974-78. But by 1993-97 the figure had risen to 89 – a hike of 58%.

on innocent parties. Its net effect may simply be to drive paedophiles underground.'

The NSPCC wants to extend a scheme in Barrow, Cumbria, that recently prevented vigilante action on a housing estate. Childwatch uses appointed adults to keep an eye on designated areas where children walk or play. The adults, called 'hidden eyes' are anonymous and look out for people acting suspiciously as they go about their business. If they see something worrying they have instant access to the police.

Graham Brooks, NSPCC area child services manager, says that although the scheme has yet to be systematically evaluated, the indications are that they work on several levels.

When a potential vigilante situation arose, Childwatch met with residents and were able to convince them that the person would be monitored, says Brooks.

Childwatch's 'hidden eyes' have found people with a record of offences against children parked outside schools. 'There is also anecdotal evidence that children's quality of life improves as parents feel happier about letting them go out and about in Childwatch areas,' says Brooks.

Child pornography

Information from ECPAT UK

The production of child pornography is often a clandestine activity enveloped in an aura of shame and secrecy. Children coerced or lured into its production may experience a great sense of confusion, disorientation and alienation. A 'modelling' effect has been observed, with the children often learning to associate sex with force and violence, and identifying with and becoming emotionally dependent on the exploiters. The simple fact that child pornography is recorded (on film, video-tape or increasingly computer disks) gives it a wide range and scope for distribution. Child pornography, however, remains a form of child abuse that can be called 'documented child abuse'.

Moreover, children not involved in the production of porno-graphic material may be forced by adults to view it, which makes pornography not only exploitative in itself, but a tool for further potential exploitation. Child pornography depicts infants as well as older children, and boys as well as girls. More than 50% of the child pornography seized by the United States depicts boys, while young girls are

the subject in Japan. It can be noticed that although child pornography can be a lucrative business for the producers, middlemen and distributors, it is often widely circulated without cost.

Technology & the Internet

The technology needed to create child pornography is generally more available in industrialised countries, but such materials are made and viewed all over the world.

Home Videos: The advent of this technology has eliminated tips that often came from staff working in commercial film processing labs which had led to many prosecutions. Video technology also now means that the 'studio' is someone's home, where perpetrators can film children with minimum risk of discovery.

More daunting, the computer has further revolutionised transmission and distribution of child pornography in the 1990s. Child pornography on the Internet has become an important issue recently because the Internet itself is developing so rapidly. Today there are estimated 153 million Internet users (NUA Internet Surveys, Jan 1999) who have on-line access to some 90 million websites (OECD, June 1998). Every month millions of new people join the Internet, only serving to fuel the increasing problem of child pornography on-line.

Why then is the Internet such a catalyst for the child pornography?

- The Internet makes pornography potentially accessible to anyone with a computer and a modem.
- Computers can scan pictures and capture video clips, and mail them electronically almost instantaneously. Detection is thwarted also, since electronic transmission helps mask the sender's identity and ensures anonymity.
- Internet Newsgroups act as bulletin boards providing an international meeting and trading environment unheard of before the Internet. This allows users to meet cheaply and regularly in order to exchange materials and develop new markets and custom.
- It removes regional and national boundaries thus propagating the scale of the problem.
- Chat rooms: The Internet provides a number of chat rooms specifically for children providing potential abusers access to many more children in an environment where they can speak to them with little fear of interruption or identification.

The abusers

There is a clear link between child Internet pornography and the abuse of children in the real world. According to a study by US Customs, 80% of all owners of child pornography are themselves abusers. They come from all types of backgrounds and the majority are men.

The victims

Children are victims of Internet pornography in two main ways. Primary concern centres on the children depicted in the images which themselves are a form of child abuse. Children who have been used in the production of material demonstrate a multitude of symptoms. Above all, guilt and shame are evident in victims, problems that are extenuated through the global availability of the material on the Internet. Secondary concern centres on those children who have access to the Internet. Such children may come into contact with illegal or harmful material which they are ill-equipped to deal with.

How then can the Internet be made safer for children?

- Encourage ISPs to report on and monitor the material which they allow web space and to encourage them to remove inappropriate sites.
- Encourage the public to use the various HOTLINES now available as a method of reporting inappropriate material. Find a UK Hotline at: www.iwf.org.uk
- Encourage parents to use Filtering Software or Filtered Search Engines which block particular sites/words.
- Encourage and support Global Legislation.

- The above information is an extract from ECPAT UK's Student Pack. See page 41 for their address details.

© ECPAT UK

Judge drives sex crime message home

By Philip Delves Broughton in New York

Sex offenders in south Texas have been ordered to put signs on their homes and vehicles advertising their presence, to the delight of locals and the horror of civil liberties groups.

'Danger. Registered Sex Offender Lives Here', reads the sign issued to 14 people in Corpus Christi, Texas. The bumper sticker reads 'Danger. Registered Sex Offender in Vehicle'. Texas law already requires that sex offenders' names and photographs be posted on the internet and in local newspapers.

However, Judge Manuel Banales ordered the offenders to display the new signs, arguing that not everyone had access to computers and newspapers. Since the order came into effect over the past week, lawyers opposing it say that one sex offender has attempted suicide, two have been evicted and the father of one has been threatened with violence.

Gerald Rogen, a lawyer representing two of the offenders, said: 'It's as if we're going back to the times of scarlet letters, public hangings and witch hunts.' Mr Rogen hopes to convince a higher court that the signs amount to a cruel and unusual punishment.

In his original ruling, Judge Banales said that he was ordering the offenders to display the signs because 'wherever they go, whatever time of day or night, we want people to be aware of where these offenders are'. The offenders targeted by Mr Banales had all been sentenced to long terms on probation rather than in prison for crimes ranging from aggravated sexual assault to indecency with a child.

He ordered less serious offenders to write letters to all of their neighbours within a three-block radius alerting them to their presence. Several counties in Texas are expected to follow Mr Banales's example after a recent incident in which a convicted sex offender lured a 12-year-old girl to his house using a pet rabbit.

Supporters of the signs say that they would have alerted the girl to the danger which awaited her.

© Telegraph Group Limited, London 2001

Child pornography and paedophilia

Information from the National Criminal Intelligence Service (NCIS)

Unlike most conventional criminals, paedophiles are not primarily motivated by financial gain. However, paedophiles often blackmail each other. The purpose of such blackmail is not to extort money but often to gain access to another paedophile's material or victims. Although most paedophiles are male, there are cases where women are involved in the sexual abuse of children. Most of these cases involve intra-family abuse, where both parents are abusing their own children.

Paedophiles prey on victims in various circumstances including children in vulnerable situations. These can include runaways and homeless children, mentally-disabled children, or children in recreational and play areas. It can also result from a deliberate abuse of trust by those employed by youth, church or care organisations, or by paedophiles who attach themselves to low-income families, gaining the trust of the parents who may then unwittingly allow the paedophile to assist in the care of the children.

Paedophiles tend to rely on networking rather than group structures. These networks are used to exchange material such as pictures, videos, stories and even victims. Paedophiles have even devised their own specialist groups, and may seek to take advantage of legitimate political or social issues to further their own interests.

The type of sexual material produced varies. Pictures range from full frontal naked images of children to images depicting children engaging in sex with adults. A considerable amount of the material is extremely explicit. Although paedophiles do produce videos, many of the more commercially produced videos actually involve adults disguised as or pretending to be children.

There is a plethora of cases documenting paedophiles' use of the Internet. These include attempts to establish networks, distribute sexual images, make use of on-line chat room facilities, publicise their stories/fantasies/'want-lists' and, in certain cases, make on-line contact with children. There have also been problems with children accessing chat rooms and coming into virtual contact with paedophiles. In addition to placing web sites on the Internet, there is evidence to suggest that some paedophiles continue to place advertisements in popular magazines. Very often these advertisements are coded and deliberately vague, offering videos and pictures. On one occasion a paedophile advertised his possession of a child.

It is currently impossible to assess the extent of abuse or the amount of obscene material produced

---

The UK's Internet Watch Foundation (IWF) provides a mechanism whereby users can report the instances of child pornography that they encounter on the Internet. Actionable complaints have grown more than fivefold in the last two

years, from 215 reports in 1997 to 1,128 in 1999. The growth, however, does not necessarily reflect a sharp increase in content, since there are also factors influencing the level of reporting: namely, the expanding number of Internet users, the higher profile of the IWF, and its adoption of a more active policy. Only a small proportion of the reported material – about 4% of actionable items in 1999 – appears to have originated in the UK. Most comes from the USA.

The presence of overt material offers opportunities for law enforcement. During 1999, monitoring of Internet sites led to a number of successful operations against child pornographers and paedophiles. Most cases relate to possession and/or distribution of child pornography, but some of those brought to court are accused of sexual abuse of children. Emerging trends show a worrying sophistication in the use of technology by some criminals.

It is currently impossible to assess the extent of abuse or the amount of obscene material produced. There are many thousands of pornographic images already on the Internet and new sites are constantly being discovered. Similarly, assessing the numbers of children abused is an extremely difficult task. If one considers the number of children who go missing in the UK each year and accepts the findings that around 30% of children in the UK are living on or around the poverty line, then there is quite a considerable pool of vulnerable children for paedophiles to target.

• The above information is an extract from the National Criminal Intelligence Service (NCIS) publication *2000 UK Threat Assessment*. See page 41 for their address details.

© *National Criminal Intelligence Service (NCIS)*

Outrage at child porn judgment

By Andrew Walker, Crime Correspondent

Detectives last night raised the spectre of Scotland becoming a safe haven for internet paedophiles after a computer engineer escaped with a £500 fine for downloading pornographic images of children, citing a controversial legal judgment that the crime was 'victimless'.

Children's charities and investigators reacted with outrage, fearing that paedophiles would head to Scotland because they could now expect more lax treatment than south of the Border, where the law provides for longer sentences and the courts also take a harder line.

Most were unaware of a crucial Appeal Court ruling in November which paved the way for yesterday's decision.

At Edinburgh Sheriff Court, James Finlay, 30, who admitted accessing indecent computer images of children between 13 March and 9 May 1999, successfully argued downloading explicit images of children was 'victimless'.

Finlay was caught during police monitoring of chat rooms, carried out as part of a larger operation which saw the collapse of an international computer paedophile ring.

Finlay's defence agent, Alex Prentice, said a recent Court of Appeal ruling described downloading pornography as a 'victimless offence' because it did not necessarily provide an incentive for those who were producing the images.

Mr Prentice argued yesterday that Finlay was obtaining already available material, one of the key tests the Appeal Court judges had stipulated. Mr Prentice added that the appellant in that earlier case, Thomas Kirk, had his jail sentence quashed. Kirk was originally sentenced at Kirkcudbright Sheriff Court to three months' jail but his punishment was reduced on appeal in November last year.

Taking into account the High Court decision yesterday, Sheriff Iain Macphail QC spared Finlay jail, fining him £500.

It was thought to be the first time a defendant had successfully used the Appeal Court judgment.

The maximum sentence in Scotland for possession of such material is two years.

In England, laws were toughened this year to a maximum 10 years and the courts there have explicitly stated children in pornographic poses are victims.

> **'The assumption that the possession of child pornography is a victimless crime is deeply questionable'**

A police source said: 'It is inconceivable to think that there is no incentive for suppliers from people downloading these images. The concern is that this country could become a safe haven for paedophiles who use the internet.'

A spokeswoman for NCH, a children's rights charity, said: 'The assumption that the possession of child pornography is a victimless crime is deeply questionable. Each image of child pornography records the scene of a crime. Anyone who produces, distributes or possesses these images is involved in crimes against children.'

Lorraine Gray, of Edinburgh-based Children 1st, said: 'Every image is a child who has been abused and by downloading that material, you are taking part in the abuse.'

Patti Ironside, the project leader of Barnado's Scotland, a member of the Children's Charities Coalition for Internet Safety, said: 'It has been well documented that pornography is used by sex offenders for compensatory fantasy as part of the pathway which may ultimately lead to sexual assault.'

Det Sgt David Reid, of Lothian and Borders Police forensic computer unit, said: 'I think the High Court finding appears to be inconsistent with opinions which have come from other jurisdictions in other countries.

'When things are shared on the internet, the users play a role as well as those who produce the images.'

Prosecutor Lindsey Anderson said Finlay accessed two chat rooms being monitored by police in England as part of an inquiry.

Finlay, of Eskbank, Dalkeith, a first offender, was placed on the sex offender register.

Kirk, a former dairyman from Springholm, Dumfries and Galloway, was found to have nearly 1,400 pornographic images on his computer, more than 700 of which featured children.

His appeal was upheld by Lords McCluskey and Weir.

The written judgment, which led to the quashing of his sentence, said: 'What the appellant did was to use his computer to access material already available in digital electronic form on the internet. Of course we recognise the exploitation and degradation of children by creating pornographic pictures of them, victimises the children.

'But nothing [Kirk] did had any direct or consequent effect upon any other person, adult or child. In that sense at least, the appellant's behaviour, consisting of operating his computer in his own home, was a "victimless offence".'

© *The Scotsman*
May 2001

Chat rooms

'Paedophile-free' chat rooms for children planned after abuse cases

'Paedophile-free' internet chat rooms are to be set up for children amid evidence that sex offenders are increasingly targeting the one million British youngsters who currently talk online.

The new electronic 'talking shops' are to be monitored by specialist 'cyber' police who are trained to investigate suspected paedophiles who use the chat rooms to lure children.

A police and Home Office study, to be published today, found that five million boys and girls aged under 16 in the UK were internet users, of whom 1.15 million made use of about 100,000 chat rooms worldwide. Detectives were shocked at the number of children hooked on the virtual meeting places.

The report *Chat Wise, Street Wise* was carried out because of concerns at the growing number of cases in which adult sex offenders posed as children on the internet to meet and abuse youngsters.

Patrick Green, 33, was jailed for five years last October after he posed as a teenage boy in a chat room and lured a 13-year-old girl to his home where he sexually abused her.

Last week, a middle-aged man alleged to have filmed sex with under-age girls he met via a chatroom was sent for trial.

Millions of children spend hours talking 'online'. Visitors can type messages and communicate with anybody else in the 'room' at the same time. People can either display messages on the screen of everyone who is logged on to the 'room' or ask another user for a more intimate, one-to-one 'chat'.

The internet service providers, who set up the chat rooms – and along with telephone companies make huge profits from them – have been criticised for refusing to monitor the contents or identify the owners.

The Internet Crime Forum, a group including representatives from the Association of Chief Police

By Jason Bennetto, Crime Correspondent

Officers, child welfare groups, internet companies, and the Home Office, are to recommend the establishment of protected children-only chat rooms.

> **Five million boys and girls aged under 16 in the UK were internet users, of whom 1.15 million made use of about 100,000 chat rooms worldwide**

Under the proposed scheme, which has the backing of the internet service providers, the cyber bulletin boards would be monitored by trained staff for inappropriate or sexually explicit language or attempts by adults to make contact with children. Sites that are protected against approaches by paedophiles will have special so-called 'kitemarks' or badges of excellence.

The Forum will also recommend that parents and children who are worried about any of the people using the chat rooms should contact a special police helpline. More officers are to be trained in dealing with offenders who attempt to abuse children via the internet. Investigations into suspected paedophiles will be co-ordinated by the High-Tech Crime Unit which is being launched at the National Crime Squad next month.

The report also notes that the police are allowed to pose as children in chat rooms when carrying out inquiries into suspected sex offenders.

Since 1995, more than 2,000 men have been convicted in America for internet sex offences following sting operations. Californian police tracked a British man who used a fake paedophile website to search for a six-year-old girl for sex.

Kenneth Lockley, 28, of Derby, went to a hotel to meet a child but was confronted by Scotland Yard officers. Lockley was jailed last year for 18 months for trying to incite an undercover officer to procure a child for sex.

However, internet sting operations by police in the UK are rare because defence barristers can argue that any evidence gathered through entrapment should be barred from court.

Children and parents are also to be given guidance about the safe use of chat rooms. These include: Never give out your e-mail or home address, phone number or the name of your school. Also, never meet someone offline unless you are sure who they are, and then in a public place with a parent or carer.

Children and parents are also to be given guidance about the safe use of chat rooms

Once a paedophile has made contact he may obtain the child's telephone number and start calling them at home or on their mobile telephone. This is usually followed by an attempt to meet the victim.

The Home Office has already published plans to increase the maximum jail sentences for paedophiles and to give police the power to intercept electronic communications made by sex offenders.

A Home Office spokesman declined to comment on the details of today's report, but said: 'We will consider the recommendations very carefully and see how we can take them forward along with the internet industry, child protection groups and the police.'

Safe surfing guide

Information from the Internet Watch Foundation

Welcome to the Internet Watch Foundation's guide to safe use of the Internet. This will help you find the best advice on the Net about its dangers for young users, and how to avoid them.

What are the dangers?
If you don't know what you should be worried about, this section explains the risks.

When your child logs on to the Internet, he or she is linking up to a vast network of computers which extends all over the globe. Children can enjoy worldwide access to material that is educational and entertaining, and to services that enable them to communicate with and learn about people from other countries and cultures.

The Internet neither belongs to nor is controlled by any one person, organisation or government. This lack of central control is sometimes portrayed as anarchic and dangerous. But on the whole it offers huge benefits. Unlike any other medium, the Internet gives everyone the chance to be a publisher – to create and publish material for people to see across the world. This is an unprecedented creative opportunity for adults and children alike.

The flip side of this is that other people may use the Internet in ways which you may find offensive, or which are actually illegal. In using the Net you need to know about the possible hazards, particularly for children, and how you can avoid them.

The Net is not a legal vacuum – the law applies online exactly as it does offline, and people who break the law are subject to investigation and prosecution. In a growing number of countries specialist hotlines have been set up to tackle the problem of illegal content.

But most material on the Internet is legal, so people have a right both to publish it and to access it. At the same time you have the right to control your own use of the Net by choosing what you personally don't want to see, or don't want your children to see.

Software tools are available to help you select the material you access, particularly on the World Wide Web. In addition, Internet Service Providers (ISPs) do vary in the range of services they offer to their subscribers, particularly in areas such as newsgroups and chat, so you can choose your ISP accordingly.

The main dangers people are concerned about can be grouped into:

Contact – the greatest danger in the virtual world is letting online contact lead to a meeting in the real world with someone who is not what they pretended to be and who poses a real physical threat. Young people must relearn the old stranger = danger messages in a new context and use the anonymity of the Net to hide their real location.

Content – legal or illegal, there are some sorts of content that might harm younger users, or that offend the values and standards that you want to apply to your children's development. You can agree the ground rules about where your children go and how they behave, and perhaps choose some software tools to help apply your rules.

Commerce – with the growth of e-commerce there are increasing concerns that in an unregulated global market place young people (and adults too!) may be exploited by dubious marketing practices or simply cheated out of their money.

Safety tips for children

Remember to stay cyber smart!

There's some great stuff on the Net, but some bad stuff too. It's important to be careful when using the Internet and remember these SMART rules!

S – Keep your personal details **Secret**. Never use your parents' credit card without their permission, and never give away your name, address, or passwords – it's like handing out the keys to your home!

M – Never **Meet** someone you have contacted in Cyberspace without your parent's/carer's permission, and then only when they can be present.

A – Don't **Accept** e-mails, open attachments or download files from people or organisations you don't really know or trust – they may contain viruses or nasty messages.

R – **Remember** that someone online may not be who they say they are. If you feel uncomfortable or worried in a chat room simply get out of there!

T – **Tell** your parent or carer if someone or something makes you feel uncomfortable or worried.

Hotline

The vast and rapidly growing range of material on the Net means that effective action is dependent on the participation of the public in reporting problems that they find.

All users of the Net are encouraged to report potentially illegal material. The 'hotlines' to receive reports are open now. Please use them.

Our first priority is child pornography. You should make a report to us if you see something which you believe to be illegal. If that is a difficult judgement for you to make, do not worry. Report it and let the Foundation make an assessment of what we should act on.

Do not hesitate if you are not sure about the law, but please do not send us reports on the sole basis that you personally find something offensive. We are concerned with the law, not personal taste or morality. We can only act on material that could be prosecuted under UK legislation.

The Foundation will assess whether reported material is potentially illegal. 'Potentially' because there are no absolute guidelines from statute or the courts and an item is not illegal until a court finds it so.

The law on child pornography is relatively clear and we are anxious to hear about any images of children, apparently under 16 years old, involved in sexual activity or posed to be sexually provocative.

Implementing this process in the UK is a positive first step, not a final solution. No single approach, in a single country, can entirely solve the problem. There are however growing indications that other countries, particularly in the European Union, will be taking similar measures and co-operating internationally.

Make a report

You can contact us 24 hours a day to let us know about material you have seen on the Internet which you consider to be potentially illegal. Our first priority is child pornography. For example, any picture of a child apparently under 16 years old, involved in sexual activity or naked and posed to be sexually provocative may be an offence under the Protection of Children Act.

Please note that there is little we can do about material which you personally find offensive if it is not liable to prosecution under UK law.

We need the following information from you:

1. A brief description of what you have seen on the Internet
2. Details of the location where you found it:

   For a Worldwide Web site this will consist of: the http:// location of the page;

   For a Usenet newsgroup article this will consist of:
   - the name of the newsgroup;
   - the title of the article;
   - the sender of the article;
   - the date of the article;
   - the name of the Internet Service Provider your account is with.
3. How to contact you if you want us to tell you what has happened with your report.

You can give us this information:
Online – visit IWF's web site at www.internetwatch.org.uk.
By e-mail – to report@iwf.org.uk
By phone – to our hot line number 08456 008844

You will be asked to make a brief recorded statement of the above information.

By fax – to our hot line fax number 01223 235921

Set out your report in the same format as the online form and send it to us.

• The above information is from the Internet Watch Foundation. See page 41 for their address details.

© Internet Watch Foundation

MY CYBER-BUDDY WANTS TO KNOW THE EXPIRY DATE OF YOUR CREDIT CARD...

New law to trap paedophiles who prowl chatrooms

By Jason Bennetto,
Crime Correspondent

Paedophiles who attempt to pick up or 'groom' children on the internet will be jailed under a controversial new law to be proposed by the Home Office today.

The 'anti-grooming' order is aimed at stopping suspected sex offenders from posing as children or teenagers in chatrooms as a ploy to meet new victims.

Ministers, the police and child welfare groups are alarmed at the increasing number of cases in which paedophiles have entrapped youngsters and later abused them after making contact on the internet and exchanging e-mails. Under the radical proposals parents, children and the police will be able to apply for a banning order against anyone suspected of using the internet to find child victims by either lying about their age or giving false personal details. If a suspect broke a court order they would face a prison term, probably of up to five years.

The police and internet service providers would be expected to monitor and trace suspects who used chatrooms and e-mails to meet children.

The proposed order is controversial because it would outlaw conduct that is merely preparatory to a crime but where the offence itself has not taken place or been attempted. The change would open the Home Office to accusations of excessive interference by trying to control the way people think and behave. Officials have admitted that the issue is complex and acknowledge that many people using the internet enjoy elements of fantasy and make-believe.

The law will be proposed today by the Home Office as part of a package of measures to protect young people using the internet, including the establishment of child-safe chatrooms.

A recent police and Home Office study found that 5 million boys and girls aged under 16 in the UK were internet users, of whom 1.15 million made use of about 100,000 chatrooms worldwide. There has been a number of cases of paedophiles making use of the electronic highway to find victims.

> *The police and internet service providers would be expected to monitor and trace suspects who used chatrooms and e-mails to meet children*

Patrick Green, 33, was jailed for five years in October after he posed as a teenage boy in an internet chatroom and lured a 13-year-old girl to his home, where he sexually abused her. Green used the internet and e-mails to conduct a two-month 'relationship' with the teenager before taking her to his flat in Buckinghamshire for sex.

Millions of children spend hours talking online in the electronic meeting places. Visitors can type messages and communicate with anybody else who is in the 'room' at the same time. People can either display messages on the screen of everyone who is logged on to the 'room' or ask another individual for a more intimate one-to-one 'chat'.

Once a paedophile has made contact he may obtain the child's telephone number and start calling them at home or on a mobile telephone and asking increasingly intimate questions. There usually follows an attempt to meet the victim.

The law already covers most paedophile activity on the internet, including producing or distributing indecent images of children under

---

Internet service providers

Children's charities welcome Demon's move against child pornography

Today children's charities welcome Demon's announcement that the Internet Service Provider (ISP) intends to block access to all newsgroups known to contain child pornography on a regular basis. The Children's Charities Coalition for Internet Safety – which consists of Barnardo's, ChildLine, NCB, NCH, NCVCCO, NSPCC and the Children's Society – applaud this significant change of policy and are now calling for all other ISPs still providing access to follow their lead.

Speaking on behalf of the coalition, NCH Internet Consultant John Carr said: 'All UK ISPs should be doing everything they can to make it as hard as possible for child pornographers to find or distribute their illegal material. We call on all ISPs to follow Demon's lead in removing newsgroups containing child pornography from their servers, thereby blocking access to some of the most horrific images available on the Net.'

© NCH Action for Children

16, asking a child to perform indecent acts, and asking a child to meet for sexual purposes. But there is no law to prevent sex offenders posing as children and trying to 'befriend' youngsters online.

Under the proposed change the police would use the civil law to obtain an 'injunction order' from a magistrate. The order would ban a named individual from specific types of conduct, such as using chatrooms and contacting children on the internet. The police would have to show that a 'reasonable person' would be concerned about the suspect's actions, such as lying about his age and intention. Breach of such an order would be a criminal offence.

The measure is part of a package of reforms published today by the Government's Task Force on Child Protection and the Internet, chaired by Lord Bassam, a Home Office minister. Other proposals include developing a 'kite-marking' scheme for chatrooms that deliver child-friendly services.

Minister unveils plan to curb Net chatrooms

By Nigel Morris

'It is pure fantasy to suppose that a predatory paedophile who has approached a child in this way will not do so again purely because of a piece of paper.

New paedophile prevention orders would close a legal loophole

'If the evidence is there to show that a paedophile is attempting to lure a child in this way, he should face the penalty of the law immediately. No second chance.' She claimed that Labour was panicking because of Tory manifesto proposals to introduce a new offence of child 'enticement'.

Plans to help prevent paedophiles preying on impressionable youngsters through the internet were unveiled yesterday by the Home Secretary, Jack Straw.

New paedophile prevention orders would close a legal loophole which allows potential abusers to build up the trust of children in internet chatrooms with non-sexual approaches. Police would be able to apply for the orders if they suspected that inappropriate approaches were being made to youngsters, with breaches carrying jail terms of up to five years. The orders would prevent any further approaches to under-16s over the Net by the named individual.

Mr Straw said: 'One of the privileges of being Home Secretary is you get behind the scenes and I have seen some images with which people at NCIS [National Criminal Intelligence Service] have been working and they are completely shocking. The images of the abuse of children are in some cases quite unbelievable.' He also said he wanted to make Britain the safest country in the world for children to surf the Net by introducing British Standard kitemarks for 'family-friendly' internet providers.

But Ann Widdecombe, the shadow Home Secretary, said the planned orders would allow paedophiles caught once to make a second attempt.

Miss Widdecombe, who accused Labour of seven times rejecting Tory proposals for tightening the law, said:

Paul Burstow, the Liberal Democrat candidate for Sutton and Cheam, welcomed the announcement but said it should have been made when he raised the issue in the Commons months ago. 'It shouldn't have taken the heat of an election campaign to do the right thing,' Mr Burstow said.

Speaking in Northampton, Mr Straw also claimed that a Tory government would mean 'huge cuts' in police numbers, equipment, technology and back-up. He said: 'Contrast that with what Labour is saying about police investment. Over the next three years we will increase police funding by over a fifth in cash terms – the equivalent of £1.6bn a year by 2004.'

He also pledged that a re-elected Labour government would tackle the 'revolving-door justice' which meant that criminals were released from prison only to reoffend.

'That is not acceptable. We need a new system which, yes, gives people the opportunity to go straight, to get off drugs, to sort out what are often chaotic lives, but one which sends out a tough message to those who continue to offend and offend again,' he said.

Mr Straw insisted that serial offenders would run a higher risk of imprisonment and serve longer sentences once locked up, while violent and sex offenders would lose their right to automatic early release.

Computer shops to block child porn on internet

By Martin Bright

High street computer retailers and software giant Microsoft are to join forces with the British police and children's charities in an unprecedented crackdown on child porn on the internet.

For the first time, PC World, Tiny and Time have agreed that they have a responsibility for child protection when they sell computers to families. All computers are to be fitted with software to filter out child pornography and 'kite marks' for child-friendly chatrooms will be introduced. The big three, which dominate the home PC market, will develop packages to block websites with adult content and access to chatrooms which paedophiles use.

Internet service providers and software manufacturers have also agreed to tighten up controls on paedophile 'newsgroups' where subscribers can exchange images and pornography about children.

It is illegal to download images of children from the internet, but not to set up a paedophile chatroom or exchange sexual fantasies involving children.

The industry was shocked into action by the 'Wonderland' case this year, in which more than a hundred paedophiles around the world were arrested and tens of thousands of images seized in an international operation led by British police.

The proposals will be announced later this week at the launch of the Government's new Internet Task Force on Child Protection, chaired by Home Office Minister Lord Bassam. The task force includes members of the industry, seven children's charities, senior police officers and Home Office officials.

Other measures being considered by the task force include tougher legislation on internet 'grooming', in which children are lured into sexual relationships with paedophiles. Actress Emily Watson, star of the film *Angela's Ashes*, will tomorrow launch a campaign on behalf of the National Society for the Prevention of Cruelty to Children warning parents to be vigilant about the dangers of the internet. The NSPCC is particularly concerned about paedophiles who persuade children to meet them after striking up an online relationship.

> **All computers are to be fitted with software to filter out child pornography and 'kite marks' for child-friendly chatrooms will be introduced**

Meanwhile, internet company V21 has responded to the huge demand for 'safe surfing' by adapting Microsoft's Internet Explorer software to block off all unsuitable sites and claims to have created the first-ever completely safe environment for children.

However, civil rights groups last night expressed concern that measures brought in to protect children from paedophiles could be used to snoop on other kinds of internet activity and censor sites that unintentionally attracted paedophiles. Caspar Bowden of the Foundation for Information Policy Research, an internet policy think tank, said: 'There is a danger that child protection concerns, fuelled by tabloid witch hunts, might develop into calls for general surveillance of private internet communications.'

The giant electrical retail Dixons group, which includes Currys and PC World, has already begun discussions with the Internet Watch Foundation, the industry's internal regulator, to develop parental guidelines for all customers of their family machines.

Dixons' corporate and public affairs director Lesley Smith said retailers recognised they had a key role in child protection. But she said: 'It is clearly in the interests of parents that we do this and we believe it is in our interests too.' She admitted that it was difficult to develop entirely foolproof technology.

The task force is thought to favour a film-style rating system developed by the Internet Content Rating Association. Mainstream websites now label their websites according to how child-friendly they are and any adult-oriented sites can be quickly filtered out by new software.

Internet Watch Foundation spokeswoman Ruth Dixon said: 'We welcome this move. The UK is ahead of the game in bringing all the stakeholders together to protect children.'

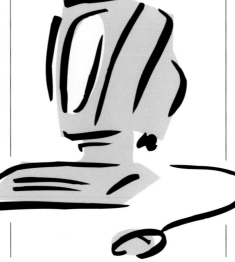

ADDITIONAL RESOURCES

You might like to contact the following organisations for further information. Due to the increasing cost of postage, many organisations cannot respond to enquiries unless they receive a stamped, addressed envelope.

Barnardo's
Tanners Lane, Barkingside
Ilford, IG6 1QG
Tel: 020 8550 8822
Fax: 020 8551 6870
E-mail: media.team@barnardos.org.uk
Web site: www.barnardos.org.uk
Barnardo's works with children, young people and their families in more than 300 projects across the county.

Calouste Gulbenkian Foundation
98 Portland Place
London, W1N 4ET
Tel: 020 7636 5313
Fax: 020 7637 3421
E-mail: info@gulbenkian.org.uk
Web site: www.gulbenkian.org.uk
Deals with social welfare and education issues.

ChildLine
2nd Floor, Royal Mail Building
50 Studd Street
London, N1 0QW
Tel: 020 7239 1000
Fax: 020 7239 1001
E-mail: reception@childline.org.uk
Web site: www.childline.org.uk
Children or young people can phone or write free of charge about problems of any kind to: ChildLine, Freepost 1111, London N1 0BR, Tel: Freephone 0800 1111.

Children 1st
41 Polwarth Terrace
Edinburgh, EH11 1NU
Tel: 0131 337 8539
Fax: 0131 346 8284
E-mail: info@children1st.org.uk
Web site: www.children1st.org.uk
Aims to protect children and young people and prevent their abuse, within the home and the community.

Children are Unbeatable!
77 Holloway Road
London, N7 8JZ
Tel: 020 7700 0627
Fax: 020 7700 1105
E-mail: info@childrenareunbeatable.org.uk
Web site: www.childrenareunbeatable.org.uk

Children are Unbeatable! supports children having the same legal protection against being hit as adults.

ECPAT UK
Thomas Clarkson House
The Stableyard, Broomgrove Road
London, SW9 9TL
Tel: 020 7501 8927
E-mail: ecpatuk@antislavery.org
Web site: www.ecpat.org.uk
ECPAT was set up by a number of agencies already working on children's rights.

EPOCH (End all Physical Punishment of Children)
77 Holloway Road
London, N7 8JZ
Tel: 020 7700 0627
Fax: 020 7700 1105
E-mail: epoch-worldwide@mcrl.poptel.org.uk
EPOCH publishes a range of leaflets, books and posters to help parents and others interested in caring for children find positive, non-violent ways of raising children.

Internet Watch Foundation (IWF)
5 Coles Lane
Oakington, CB4 5BA
Tel: 01223 237700
Fax: 01223 235870
E-mail: admin@iwf.org.uk
Web site: www.internetwatch.org.uk
IWF was launched to address the problem of illegal material on the Internet, with particular reference to child pornography.

Kidscape Campaign for Children's Safety
2 Grosvenor Gardens
London, SW1W 0DH
Tel: 020 7730 3300
Fax: 020 7730 7081
E-mail: contact@kidscape.org.uk
Web site: www.kidscape.org.uk
Works to prevent the abuse of children through education programmes involving parents and teachers. Produces a wide range of books, videos and leaflets on child-related issues including bullying and child abuse.

National Criminal Intelligence Service (NCIS)
PO Box 8000
London, SE11 5EN
Tel: 020 7238 8000
Web site: www.ncis.gov.uk
NCIS works to provide leadership and excellence in criminal intelligence to combat serious and organised crime.

NCH Action for Children
85 Highbury Park
London, N5 1UD
Tel: 020 7704 7000
Fax: 020 7226 2537
Web site: www.nchafc.org.uk
Works to improve the lives of Britain's most vulnerable children and young people.

NSPCC – National Society for the Prevention of Cruelty to Children
National Centre, 42 Curtain Road
London, EC2A 3NH
Tel: 020 7825 2500
Fax: 020 7825 2525
E-mail: info@nspcc.org.uk
Web site: www.nspcc.org.uk
Has a network of Child Protection Teams and projects to protect children from abuse. Operates the Child Protection Helpline on 0800 800 500.

Scottish Women's Aid
Norton Park, 57 Albion Road
Edinburgh, EH7 5QY
Tel: 0131 475 2372
Fax: 0131 475 2384
E-mail: swa2swa-l.demon.co.uk
Website: www.scottishwomensaid.co.uk
Provides information, support and safe refuge for women, children and young people who are experiencing or have experienced domestic abuse.

YoungMinds
102-108 Clerkenwell Road
London, EC1M 5SA
Tel: 020 7336 8445
Fax: 020 7336 8446
E-mail: enquiries@youngminds.org.uk
Web site: www.youngminds.org.uk
YoungMinds is committed to improving the mental health of all children and young people.

INDEX

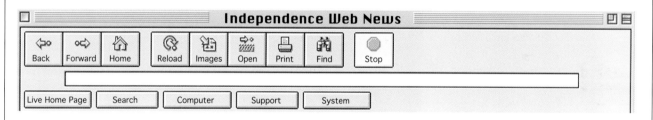

★★★★★

The Internet has been likened to shopping in a supermarket without aisles. The press of a button on a Web browser can bring up thousands of sites but working your way through them to find what you want can involve long and frustrating on-line searches.

ChildLine
www.childline.org.uk
ChildLine is the UK's free national helpline for children and young people in trouble or danger. Click on the Children and Young People button and go to the Factsheets link of their web site for a range of useful information and a factsheet on child abuse.

NSPCC – National Society for the Prevention of Cruelty to Children
www.nspcc.org.uk
Clicking on the Full Stop icon on their home page will take you to information about their Full Stop Campaign including information on The Child in the Community and Tackling the Problem. Entering 'child abuse' in the search link brings up a listing of alternative information.

And unfortunately many sites contain inaccurate, misleading or heavily biased information. Our researchers have therefore undertaken an extensive analysis to bring you a selection of quality Web site addresses.

Internet Watch Foundation (IWF)
www.internetwatch.org.uk
The Internet Watch Foundation (IWF) was launched in 1996 to address the problem of illegal material on the internet, with particular reference to child pornography. Broadly, IWF aims to enhance the enormous potential of the internet to inform, educate, entertain and conduct business by: hindering the use of the internet to transmit illegal material, particularly child pornography; encouraging the classification of legal material on the Net in order to enable users to customise the nature of their experience of the Net to their own requirements.

ACKNOWLEDGEMENTS

The publisher is grateful for permission to reproduce the following material.

While every care has been taken to trace and acknowledge copyright, the publisher tenders its apology for any accidental infringement or where copyright has proved untraceable. The publisher would be pleased to come to a suitable arrangement in any such case with the rightful owner.

Chapter One: Child Abuse

Child abuse, © Children 1st, *The facts*, © NSPCC 2000, *1m children 'have suffered abuse inside the family'*, © The Daily Mail, November 2000, *Child abuse*, © ChildLine, *Who are the abusers?*, © Scottish Women's Aid, *Signs and symptoms*, © Kidscape, *The causes of cruelty*, © NSPCC 2000, *When I was a little girl*, © Guardian Newspapers Limited 2000, *Survey reveals widespread child abuse*, © Guardian Newspapers Limited 2000, *Child protection*, © NCH Action for Children, *Child protection*, © Crown copyright is reproduced with the permission of the Controller of Her Majesty's Stationery Office (HMSO), *Child maltreatment in the UK*, © NSPCC 2000, *The extent of violence involving children*, © Calouste Gulbenkian Foundation, *No child's play*, © Guardian Newspapers Limited 2000, *Child sexual abuse*, © Barnardo's, *How the police fail 'at risk' youngsters*, © The Daily Mail, January 2001, *Sexually abused?*, © YoungMinds, *Child protection statistics*, © Crown copyright is reproduced with the permission of the Controller of Her Majesty's Stationery Office (HMSO), *Kidscape keepsafe code*, © Kidscape, *Dealing with suspected abuse*, © NSPCC 2000, *Government to allow smacking by childminders*, © 2001 The Independent Newspaper (UK) Ltd, *Internet ban puts children in their place*, © Telegraph Group Limited, London 2001, *Childminders and smacking*, © Crown copyright is reproduced with the permission of the Controller of Her Majesty's Stationery Office (HMSO), *What's wrong with smacking?*, © EPOCH, *Why should physical punishment be banned?*, © Children are Unbeatable!, *Hitting people is wrong*, © EPOCH.

Chapter Two: Paedophiles

Protect children from paedophiles!, © Kidscape, *Eyes wide open*, © Guardian Newspapers Limited 2000, *Child pornography*, © ECPAT UK, *Judge drives sex crime message home*, © Telegraph Group Limited, London 2001, *Child pornography and paedophilia*, © National Criminal Intelligence Service (NCIS), *Outrage at child porn judgment*, © The Scotsman, May 2001, *Chat rooms*, © 2001 The Independent Newspaper (UK) Ltd, *Safe surfing guide*, © Internet Watch Foundation (IWF), *New law to trap paedophiles who prowl chatrooms*, © 2001 The Independent Newspaper (UK) Ltd, *Internet service providers*, © NCH Action for Children, *Minister unveils plan to curb Net chatrooms*, © 2001 The Independent Newspaper (UK) Ltd, *Computer shops to block child porn on internet*, © Guardian Newspapers Limited 2001.

Photographs and illustrations:

Pages 1, 11, 17, 21, 28, 35: Pumpkin House, pages 5, 7, 13, 23, 25, 30, 37: Simon Kneebone.

Craig Donnellan
Cambridge
September, 2001